# OUTLINES OF
# ASCETICISM
## FOR SEMINARIANS

By F. J. Remler, C.M.

Kenrick Seminary, St. Louis, Mo.

Catholic Authors Press

Outlines of Asceticism for Seminarians
Copyright © 1939 F.J. Remler
Reprinted 2007 Catholic Authors Press
All rights reserved
ISBN:978-0-9782985-9-3

*Imprimi potest.*
Marshall F. Winne, C. M.,
Provincialis.

*Nihil obstat.*
F. J. Holweck,
Censor librorum.

*Imprimatur.*
✠ Joannes J. Glennon,
Archiepiscopus Sti. Ludovici.

16. Nov., 1938.

# TABLE OF CONTENTS

III

# INTRODUCTION

"We turn our thoughts and our words, with very special tenderness, to you who are still in your studies for the priesthood; and urge you from the depth of our heart to prepare yourselves with all seriousness for the great task to which God calls you. You are the hope of the Church and of the people, who look for so much, or rather everything, to you. For to you they look for that living and life-giving knowledge of God and of Jesus Christ in which is eternal life.

"In piety, purity, humility, obedience, discipline and study strive to make yourselves priests after the heart of God. We assure you that in the task of fitting yourselves for the priesthood by solid virtue and learning, no care, no diligence, no energy can be too great; because upon it so largely depend all your future apostolic labors. See to it that, on the day of your ordination to the priesthood, the Church find you in fact such as she wishes you to be, that is, 'replenished with heavenly wisdom, irreproachable in life and established in the ways of grace'; so that 'the sweet odor of your life may be a delight to the Church of Christ, that both by word and by good example you may build the house, that is, the family of God.'

"Only thus can you continue the glorious traditions of the Catholic priesthood and hasten that most auspicious hour when it will be given to all humanity to enjoy the fruits of the peace of Christ in the Kingdom of Christ."

— Encyclical of Pius XI, "Ad Catholici Sacerdotii."

The Holy Father's plea is for holiness among priests and priests-to-be. They must be ascetics, i. e., men who by proper training and drilling and exercise have become proficient in the supernatural life. But this training, like all other training, must be systematic and carried out according to fixed principles and rules. In the absence of this, there may be an accumulation of spiritual exercises, performed more or less at random, but not a systematic development of the supernatural life in all its relations to God.

This little volume represents an attempt to place before seminarians in a concise and condensed form — in a sort of bird's-eye view — the principles, rules and practices of the supernatural life that they are called upon to study in larger works of Ascetic Theology and that are explained to them in spiritual conferences and lectures. As such it should prove to be helpful to them in trying to master so important a science, which unfortunately is only too often looked upon as something mysterious and mystifying, and, because thus misunderstood, is considered to be of no great importance. And yet it is nothing else than the necessary Science of the Saints.

May the Great High Priest give His blessing to this little work, that it may be profitable to all seminarians who are earnestly striving to be truly Christlike now, that later as priests they may be "Other Christs" in deed and in truth.

The Author.

# CHAPTER I

## SACERDOTAL PERFECTION

The sublimity of the sacerdotal state demands the highest attainable degree of sanctity in the priest. Hence earnest application to the work of self-sanctification or the acquisition of perfection is obligatory on every young man called to be a priest—another Christ. Such a one is under greater obligation to become perfect than one who lives under the vows of religion. A religious is obliged to strive after perfection all his life; a young man who is called to be a priest is meant to be perfect on the day of his ordination.

"If you had the purity of an angel and the sanctity of St. John the Baptist, you would not be worthy to handle this Sacrament." If the future priest cannot attain to this exalted degree of holiness — which is beyond his reach — he must at least consider himself obliged to aim at reaching that degree which is proportionate to the special measure of grace offered him by God in view of his vocation to the sacred priesthood.

The young seminarian should therefore often reflect seriously on the following instructions of our divine Lord: "Be you perfect, as also your heavenly Father is perfect" (Matt. 5:48); "I have given you an example, that as I have done, so you do also" (John 13:15); "In this is My Father glorified, that you bring forth very much fruit, and become My disciples" (John 15:8); "As My Father hath loved Me, I also have loved you. Abide in My love" (John

15:9); "You are My friends if you do the things that I command you" (John 15:14). "You have not chosen Me, but I have chosen you, and have appointed you that you should go and should bring forth fruit, and your fruit should remain" (John 15:16).

Perfection demands that the future priest must endeavor to become Christlike in all things — in thought, word and action. "Let this mind be in you which was also in Christ Jesus" (Phil. 2:5).

To acquire this perfection, the seminarian must strive to attain these two objects:

**I. Freedom from all deliberate sin, both mortal and venial.**

**II. Proficiency in the practice of the various Christian virtues.**

### I. FREEDOM FROM SIN.

This is attained by two means: 1. Perfect conversion from sin; 2. Avoidance of sin, both mortal and venial.

### 1. PERFECT CONVERSION FROM SIN.

1. **A very sincere and sorrowful Confession of one's past sins**; also a great care at all times to receive the Sacrament of Penance with sincerity and earnestness.

2. **The spirit and virtue of Penance**, which may be practised by the following means:

   a) The habit of making many fervent acts of contrition.
   b) The resolute avoidance of all sinful and dangerous pleasures.
   c) The faithful observance of the laws of fast and abstinence.
   d) Self-denial and mortification in lawful pleasures.
   e) Voluntary acts of self-denial and mortification.

f) Means thereto: daily duties, observance of rules, silence, weather, table, companions, restricting one's indulgence in smoking, delicacies, comforts, luxuries, etc.

## 2. AVOIDANCE OF SIN.

This regards mortal sin, wilful occasions of sin, deliberate venial sin and indeliberate venial sin.

1. Mortal sin must be considered entirely in the light of faith, and avoided at any cost.

2. Wilful occasions of sin. One who would avoid sin must also resolutely avoid the occasions thereof. Such are:

a) Dangerous reading.
b) Improper conversations.
c) Dangerous amusements, and such as are unbecoming a cleric: theatres, movies, resorts, races, gambling, parties, dances, etc.

3. Deliberate venial sin is incompatible with perfect love of God. Some of the more common venial sins are:

a) Internal:
   Pride, vanity, envy, idle thoughts, wilful distractions, unkind thoughts and judgments.

b) External:
   Haughtiness, disrespect for authority, disobedience, criticism, murmuring, uncharitable speech, unkind actions, untruthfulness, lying, deceitfulness, waste of time, irreverence in sacred places, conduct unbecoming a gentleman.

4. Indeliberate venial sin.* Strive earnestly to diminish the number of such sins. Repent promptly of those committed and make atonement for them.

---

*Deliberate venial sins* are such as are committed *with* full advertence and full consent. *Indeliberate venial sins* are such as are committed *without* full advertence and full consent, but proceed from surprise, precipitancy, impetuosity, etc.

**Rule of Conduct:**

Resolutely avoid whatever you know to be displeasing to our Lord, even if it cannot be called a sin. Perfection demands the avoidance of imperfections and faults as much as possible.

## II. PRACTICE OF VIRTUE.

A life of perfection requires the persevering practice of the various Christian virtues. There are the **Theological, Cardinal** and **Moral** virtues.

### 1. THEOLOGICAL VIRTUES.

1. **Faith.** This must be developed and perfected by:
   a) Prayer, meditation, pious reflections, study, spiritual reading, conferences, etc.
   b) Hindrances to be avoided: levity or thoughtlessness; want of reverence for sacred persons and things; dangerous reading; materialistic views of life; liberalism.
   c) The aim must be to make one's faith a living one, i. e., to shape one's conduct according to the precepts and maxims of the Gospel.

2. **Hope.** This must be cultivated diligently as to:
   a) The forgiveness of one's past sins.
   b) The grant of the graces needed for developing one's vocation.
   c) The graces needed in time of temptation.
   d) Each one should strive to acquire the perfection of the virtue of Hope, which is Confidence.

3. **Charity** in its two branches: **love of God and love of neighbor.** In regard to God:
   a) Striving to love Him "with one's whole heart, whole soul, whole mind and whole strength," both affectively, by making many acts of love, and effectively, by faithfully doing His will in all things: "If you love Me, keep My commandments."

4

b) Seeking to cultivate an ardent personal love for Jesus Christ. "As the Father hath loved Me, I also have loved you; abide in My love."

c) Means thereto: frequent meditation on the Gospel text; pious reflections; devotion to the Blessed Sacrament, the Sacred Heart, the Passion.

d) Love of neighbor: first degree, striving to love everyone as you love yourself; second degree, striving to love everyone as Christ loves you.

e) Consists in good will to all persons; personal service; kindness in thought, word and action; bearing with others' faults; forgiveness of all injuries; love of enemies.

## 2. CARDINAL VIRTUES.

1. **Prudence**, "the guide of all the virtues": a virtue dictating what, in a particular case, is best to be done, to act according to God's will. It embraces: consideration of the past, circumspection of present circumstances, foresight of the future; impartiality, docility, sagacity, skill, caution, fidelity. Opposed to it are: cunning, deceit, over-solicitude, anxiety, rashness, inconstancy, negligence.

2. **Justice**: a virtue leading us to give to everyone what is his due, as to conduct and property. Its divisions are:

a) Legal, to give what is due to the state and society.

b) Commutative, to give what is due as a price, value, wage.

c) Distributive, to give honors and rewards according to merit, rank.

d) Vindictive, to award punishment according to the fault.

It embraces: **toward God**, religion, piety, atonement for sin; **toward neighbors**, love, reverence and obedience toward parents; respect, obedience and loyalty toward superiors; affability, generosity toward equals; instruction, correction and compassion toward inferiors; toward ourselves, care of mind and body, truth, purity, honor.

3. **Fortitude:** a virtue which moderates the passions, especially fear, and directs our conduct in bearing difficulties for God.

Its office is: to moderate fear, audacity, sorrow; to enable us to face difficulties with courage, as sickness, pain, trials, and to bear them patiently; to strengthen us for death, even martyrdom.

4. **Temperance:** a virtue implying moderation in all things.

It embraces: abstinence from excessive use of food; sobriety, in the use of intoxicating drinks; chastity, regulating carnal pleasure; mortification, modesty, humility, meekness, clemency, politeness.

### 3. MORAL VIRTUES.

1. **The Virtues of the Eight Beatitudes:**
a) Poverty of spirit: love of poverty, contentment with little, detachment from earthly goods.
b) Meekness: gentleness, kindness.
c) Mourning: the spirit of penance; reparation and atonement.
d) Hunger and thirst for justice: ardent desire for holiness and perfection.
e) Mercifulness: compassion, helpfulness.
f) Purity of heart: chastity, freedom from sin.
g) Peacefulness: bearing and forgiving injuries.
h) Willingness to suffer persecution for the love of God and the practice of virtue. "All that will live godly in Christ Jesus shall suffer persecution" (2 Tim. 3:12).

2. **The Twelve Fruits of the Holy Ghost:**
a) Charity: love of God and man.
b) Joy: by reason of baptismal innocence or perfect repentance.

6

c) Peace: with God, neighbor and self.
d) Patience: bearing with faults and defects of others; enduring sufferings with resignation.
e) Benignity: kindness, gentleness, affability.
f) Goodness: always seeking to do good to others.
g) Long-suffering: the perfection of patience.
h) Mildness: in judging the actions of others.
i) Fidelity: truthfulness; conscientious performance of all duties.
j) Modesty: custody and restraint of the senses.
k) Continency: self-denial, control of the passions.
l) Chastity: purity of soul and body.

3. Special Virtues:

a) Humility. Without this there is no growth in holiness. Pride shuts out the love of God.
b) Spirit of prayer. All graces must be secured by means of prayer.
c) Self-denial. "If anyone will come after Me, let him deny himself."

Rule of Conduct:

Generously do whatever you know to be pleasing to our Lord, or whatever He asks you to do, even though this should involve painful sacrifices.

Recommendations:

Be severely in earnest in guarding against the following obstacles to sacerdotal perfection:

1. Thoughtless and slovenly prayers — the Sign of the Cross, genuflections, meal prayers, Rosary, Mass, etc.

2. Routine and unprofitable Confessions, due to a lack of faith, earnestness and sincerity. Signs: no amendment, no correction of sinful habits, no endeavor to avoid venial sins.

3. Routine and fruitless Communions; failing to "trade" with the graces of the Sacrament, i. e., failing to produce fruits of virtue proportionate to the

graces received. It is not enough to receive the graces of Holy Communion; it is necessary to turn these graces to good account.

4. Abuse and bad use of grace. This acts on the soul as creeping paralysis acts on the body. It gradually leads to the spiritual death of the soul by mortal sin.

Perfection requires:

1. A constant and firm endeavor to avoid all manner of wilful sin, even the smallest.

2. A permanent disposition to practise the various divine and moral virtues.

3. The maintenance of this disposition in a state of constant activity.

"He that hath My commandments and keepeth them, he it is that loveth Me" (John 14:21).

# CHAPTER II

## PARTICULAR VIRTUES

That you as a seminarian may be able to develop in yourself the supernatural life to the highest possible degree, and acquire the perfection of virtue and holiness that God demands of you by reason of your sublime vocation, you must seek to practise faithfully the following special virtues.

### 1. THE SPIRIT OF A LIVING FAITH.

This is the necessary foundation of a true supernatural life. To cultivate it, take up the Gospels and read with great attention and much reflection the words of our divine Lord recorded there, imagining that they are addressed to you personally. Study their meaning carefully and earnestly seek to reduce to practice what you have learned. Try to live as no doubt you would if our divine Lord deigned to appear to you and give you these same instructions. (See Chapter III.)

In the next place, make sustained and persevering efforts to sanctify all your daily actions, paying special attention to the perfect performance of the little ones, such as: the Sign of the Cross, genuflections, aspirations, prayers before and after class, before and after meals, visits to the Blessed Sacrament, etc. (Compare: the bricks and stones that go to make up a beautiful building.) Make sure to unite all your actions most intimately with those of Jesus Christ, and to maintain at all times a very pure intention.

(Compare: the mingling of a few drops of water with a large quantity of wine.)

Lastly, remember that true devotion consists in three things: 1. Fidelity to all your spiritual exercises and all other duties; 2. Completeness and perfection in the manner of performing them; 3. Purity of intention, by which they are done solely for the honor and glory of God. (See Chapter XIV.)

## 2. PURIFICATION OF THE SOUL.

The second requisite for sacerdotal perfection is the purification of the soul from past sins and the earnest endeavor to keep it free from all deliberate sins for the future. This is done by means of frequent, sincere and sorrowful confession and the cultivation of an abiding sorrow for sin and of the spirit of penance. As to confession, you must carefully guard against making it in a routine fashion. And as to the spirit of penance, you must constantly seek to practise it by self-denial and mortification in the little things of daily life, e. g., smoking, delicacies, silence, observance of rules, promptness, obedience, good use of time, bearing with the defects of others, enduring disagreeable things without murmuring and complaining, etc.

## 3. THE SPIRIT OF HUMILITY.

In the third place you must live in the conviction that you cannot persevere in the grace and love of God unless you are possessed of true humility of heart. That you may acquire this necessary virtue, try to see yourself as you are in the sight of God — in the order of nature and of grace, you are utterly dependent on Him for all you are and all you have; and by reason of your many sins, you are a pardoned criminal. Cultivate a living faith in this declaration of our Lord: "He that humbleth himself shall be exalted, but he that exalteth himself shall be humbled." Try to accept humiliations in the spirit of penance and atonement for your sins. Also remember that humility is essential for the practice of perfect fraternal charity; he who is not truly humble can not be truly charitable. (See Chapter IX.)

## 4. FRATERNAL CHARITY.

The virtue of fraternal charity is a "conditio sine qua non" of perfect love of God. Never forget that every act of uncharitableness is directed, not so much against the person of your neighbor, as against the person of our divine Saviour. Study to practise this virtue in two ways: first, always try to love everyone as you love yourself; second, try to love everyone as Christ loves you. Cultivate it in thought, word and action; by esteem, kindness, patience, meekness, helpfulness, the spirit of forgiveness and prayer. By trying to act the part of a gentleman at all times and faithfully observing the rules of Christian politeness, you have numerous opportunities every day to practise this virtue in a very high degree of perfection. Remember too that this virtue is essential for success in your future priestly work: "He that has not charity for his neighbor is unfit for the work of preaching the Gospel" (St. Gregory).

## 5. PERSONAL LOVE OF JESUS CHRIST.

An ardent personal love of Jesus Christ is indispensably necessary to one who desires to become a good priest. To cultivate this, imitate the Apostles who after the Ascension often thought of Him and recalled His life, words and actions. Frequently recall the remembrance of Him by means of fervent aspirations, reflection and meditation on His life and teaching; by making many acts of love; by attention and recollection in prayer; by an ardent devotion to the Blessed Sacrament, fervent visits, devout reception of Holy Communion, etc. Try to realize that He desires that you love Him with the love of friendship: "I will not now call you servants; . . . but I have called you friends" (John 15:15). Hence strive to avoid most carefully every wilful sin, even the smallest. Do not forget that every such sin is an insult offered to Him. The rule of friendship demands that you always seek to do what you know to be pleasing to Him, and resolutely to avoid whatever you know to be displeasing, even though this should involve painful sacrifices. "You are My friends if you do the things that I command you"; "If you love Me, keep My commandments."

To this devotion to our divine Lord you must join a very fervent and childlike devotion to the Blessed Virgin Mary, the Mother of the Priest. Let your motto be: "All for Jesus through Mary."(See Chapter XV.)

## 6. STRENGTH OF CHARACTER.

While in the seminary you must strive perseveringly to acquire what is so essential for a priest who desires to promote God's interests in the world, namely, strength of character. For this purpose you must seek to know what you have to do, and then do it faithfully, even in the face of difficulties — from a sense of duty, for the love of God, and for your own sanctification. Train yourself to habits of right living and learn to disregard human respect and the fear of men's opinions. Never do anything wrong to escape the censure of men; and never seek to please men at the risk of displeasing God. Never forget that you must render your account to God and not to men. (See Chapter IV.)

# CHAPTER III

## REALIZING THE SUPERNATURAL

It is of supreme importance for the seminarian to have a correct understanding and keen realization of what is meant by the supernatural life. Without this he will never be able to acquire solid virtue and a high degree of sanctity. He is like a man walking in twilight; everything around him is hazy and blurred.

He who has not a clear knowledge of the supernatural cannot have right ideas about such important truths as: union with Christ, the value of grace, the evil and malice of sin, the danger of abuse of grace, the Real Presence, the Passion of Christ, the need of penance and self-denial, the necessity of prayer, the malice of Satan, the evil of worldliness, and above all, the dignity and sublimity of the sacerdotal state and its responsibilities and duties as well as the obligation of holiness it carries with it.

One reason for this lies in the fact that the supernatural is what the word implies — above the natural, and outside the reach of material perception. It does not fall under the five senses; it cannot be seen with the eyes, tasted with the tongue nor touched with the hand. The truths and laws of the supernatural life cannot for this reason be observed, studied and applied like those of the natural order; as, for example, those of physical health, or of the natural sciences, like magnetism and gravitation.

From this it follows that these truths easily escape our attention to a greater or less degree, sometimes even altogether, and to that extent fail to influence our life and conduct. Hence persons who have not cultivated the realization of the supernatural by the exercise of a living faith quite commonly lead a mere natural life despite the faith that was implanted in their souls in Baptism. Instead of having their thoughts and aspirations fixed on heaven, they grovel on the earth; "they are of the earth, earthly."

To counteract this difficulty which, while it lasts, is an insurmountable obstacle to holiness, the seminarian must be firmly determined to cultivate the **habit of living by faith,** that is, of making the teachings of Jesus Christ realities to himself. He must seek to understand the truths of the Gospel in the mind of Christ, and acquire the facility of realizing the invisible and intangible things of God as though he saw them with his bodily eyes and touched them with his hands as St. Thomas did the marks of the nails and spear in our Saviour's glorified Body.

There are several general principles suggested by faith that should always be present to the seminarian and direct his attitude toward the invisible truths of God and his conduct in regard to them. Convinced that there is no appeal from the words and declarations of Christ, he must seek to regulate all his thoughts, words and actions by them, and thus become conformed to His divine Master and Exemplar.

The following particular points are suggested for his special consideration:

1. He should continually remember that God is present as the witness and judge of all his actions, even his most secret ones.

2. He should think of Christ not as a historical Personage, but as an intimate and loving Friend, with Whom he can converse always, and especially when visiting Him in the Blessed Sacrament.

3. Sin must not be regarded as a trivial and inconsequential thing, but as a treachery and outrage against God which will have most tragical results.

4. In temptation he should remember the reward of heaven and the terrors of hell as if they were to follow immediately upon his decision.

5. As for riches and poverty, affliction and pleasure, humiliation and honor, labor and idleness, he should recall the words and example of Christ and bear himself as He did.

6. He should remember that life is short, that death is close at hand and the next life eternal; that the world is worth nothing except as a preparation for heaven; that strict retribution awaits every action; and that God is the only object worthy of man's desire, service and love.

"The just man liveth by faith."

# CHAPTER IV

## FORMATION OF CHARACTER

Besides striving to acquire sanctity and learning, the future priest must diligently attend to the forming of a strong character. A priest without character is like a vibrating reed; one with character like the sturdy oak. Such a one will be perfectly faithful to duty, and also excel in the so-called social virtues elevated to the supernatural order.

### 1. CHARACTER.

Character is life dominated by principles as distinguished from life dominated by mere impulses from within, and mere circumstances from without. This is another way of saying that he must acquire self-control, so that under all circumstances he will act according to the dictates of faith and conscience and the requirements of Christian refinement of manners. **Principles** are conceptions deeply rooted in the mind, elevated into standards of judgment, taste, feeling and action, and consistently applied to life. A collection of principles covering all departments of life constitutes an **ideal**. A man of principles is therefore a man with an ideal. (There can be people of good and also of bad character according as their principles and ideals are good or bad.)

It is therefore very important for the seminarian, first, to acquaint himself with the best and noblest ideal; secondly, to get that ideal stamped into his mind in the concrete form of sound principles; thirdly, so firmly to establish the habit of acting according to those principles that it will last for the rest of his life.

## 2. THE SEMINARIAN'S IDEAL.

For the seminarian this ideal consists, first, in a living faith in Jesus Christ and His teachings; secondly, in personal loyalty and ardent love toward Him; thirdly, in a full surrender of his will to the will of Christ; and fourthly, in the acceptance of Christ as a living, heaven-sent model to which it is his highest ambition to conform.

His model and ideal is therefore Christ as manifested to him through the Gospels. This ideal has the advantage of appearing before him ready-made, in a concrete and living form, and is all the more calculated to influence him on that account. Let him then study attentively the life, sayings and actions of Christ as recorded in the Gospels and apply to his own life what he discovers there. This will enable him to produce in himself what the Apostles were able to do by reason of their companionship with Him.

There is no situation in which he will not be able to reduce Christ's example to practice in one way or another and thus succeed in making his whole life and conduct Christlike and transforming himself into an image and likeness of his divine Master.

## 3. A MATTER OF SELF-TRAINING.

Character cannot be imposed from without. The formation of character is essentially a matter of self-training. All real training is self-training. No man has the power to force the will or to encroach on the dispositions of another. No man can form a

17

good character in another, any more than he can form a good musician or orator or painter. Seminary authorities cannot form good priests, in the sense that they can work miracles with unwilling subjects. They can help by advice, direction, encouragement; but they can go no further. Hence success in forming priests of strong character will be achieved only in so far as seminarians take their own training in hand according to the lines laid out before them.

## 4. REFINEMENT OF MANNERS.

Besides training himself in the faithful discharge of all his duties — a most important item in a priest's life — the seminarian must apply himself perseveringly to the formation of those habits of genuinely Christian courtesy and politeness and refinement of manners which are indispensable for a fruitful priestly ministry. A delicate regard for the rights and feelings of others is the refinement of Christian charity. With it the priest becomes a great power for good; without it he does much harm to souls, even to the extent of their eternal perdition. Meekness, kindness, gentleness, politeness, attract souls to him and to God; impatience, harshness, scolding, boorishness and vulgarity, want of civility, repel them and make them conceive a dislike for the religion he represents.

To cultivate this necessary refinement of manners, the seminarian must apply himself to the task of acquiring proper control of the spontaneous movements of the body. This covers all that goes to the make-up of proper deportment — graceful gait and carriage, "clerical gravity," repose of manner, the habit of sitting still, restraint of the eyes, avoiding uncontrolled outbursts of laughter — "the loud laugh that speaks the vacant mind" — boisterous talking, shouting, yelling, whistling, interrupting others in their speech, using slang and vulgar expressions, and

18

other such offensive actions, all of which indicate a lack of refinement and a want of self-discipline and self-control. "The attire of the body, and the laughter of the teeth, and the gait of the man show what he is" (Ecclus. 19:27).

"To be a perfect gentleman is one of the greatest aids to being a perfect Christian"; whereas "vulgarity is the greatest of vices, because it is composed of so many small ones" (Cardinal Newman).

# CHAPTER V

## PRAYER

What the exercise of breathing is to the life of the body, that the exercise of prayer is to the supernatural life of the soul. Without breathing, the physical life must cease; without prayer, the soul must lose what grace and union with God it possesses. Neglect of prayer spells doom to the soul. Hence the need of learning to pray well. "Lord, teach me to pray" should be the constant fervent prayer of the seminarian and of the priest.

### 1. DEFINITION.

The following is a comprehensive definition of prayer: An elevation of our soul to God to offer Him our homage of adoration, praise and thanksgiving, and to ask for His favors in order to grow in holiness for His glory.

### 2. FORMS OF PRAYER.

1. Prayer of Worship, which includes:

a) Adoration and praise. Our first and foremost duty is to acknowledge God's supreme dominion over us and our absolute dependence on Him.

b) Thanksgiving. We are obliged to everlasting gratitude to Him as our greatest Benefactor, to Whom we owe all we are and all we have, both in the order of nature and in that of grace.

20

c) Reparation or expiation. This is made necessary by the sins we have committed against Him, which must be atoned for either here or in purgatory.

**2. Prayer of Petition.** God knows our wants and needs perfectly, and therefore need not be told of them; but He has decreed that we obtain what we require only by means of humble, earnest, trusting and persevering petition. This is for the exercise of humility and the acknowledgment of our utter dependence on Him; it is only pride and presumption not to comply with this condition of obtaining what is needed.

It is a common mistake to think of prayer mainly in the form of petition for favors, and not in the form of worship. For this reason many pay little attention to adoration, praise and thanksgiving, though this is the more noble and more perfect kind of prayer, and the kind that will be practised in heaven for all eternity. Souls that aspire to holiness must seek to practise it as perfectly as possible. This in turn will insure God's greater readiness and liberality in answering their prayers of petition.

## 3. VARIETIES OF PRAYER.

**1. Mental prayer.** This consists in a silent intercourse or converse of the soul with God. Every interior act of the mind or of the heart that tends to unite us to God, such as: recollection, consideration, reasoning, self-examination, the loving thought of God, contemplation, a longing of the heart for God — all these may be called mental prayer. (See next chapter.)

**2. Vocal prayer.** This is prayer in word or act. Man, composed of soul and body, must also employ his body and its senses for the glory of God. Hence the need of vocal expression of interior sentiments

21

and reverence in bodily posture, such as folding the hands, kneeling, standing, bowing, etc.

**3. Private prayer.** Every man owes to God the homage of prayer independently of others, though he must also join with others for public worship. "Pray always," "Pray without ceasing," etc., apply largely to the habit or virtue of prayer which is to be exercised by every devout Christian.

**4. Public prayer.** In the Catholic Church great importance attaches to prayer which is offered by the faithful in groups and communities in such a way that "with one mind and with one mouth" they "may glorify God and the Father of our Lord Jesus Christ." Public prayer has a special efficacy with God, according to our Lord's declaration: "Where there are two or three gathered together in My name, there I am in the midst of them." Hence the great value of family prayers, of the public services in our churches, of taking part in solemnities, processions, etc.

## 4. NECESSITY OF PRAYER.

God has made prayer an absolute condition for the bestowal of the graces we need for our sanctification and the attainment of salvation. Through prayer we can obtain every grace necessary for the success of the work that is to be done by us for God; without prayer all our efforts are foredoomed to failure.

Every lapse from grace, every case of priestly apostasy, every case of eternal damnation, can be traced back to the neglect, or to the bad performance, of prayer. Prayer is as necessary for obtaining grace and for perseverance in grace as an aqueduct is for a city's water supply or a properly adjusted system of wiring for electric illumination. Destroy the aqueduct and there is a shortage of water; cut the current-carrying wires and there will be darkness; neglect prayer and there will be spiritual disaster.

# CHAPTER VI

## THE EXERCISE OF MEDITATION

For the supernatural life to be properly maintained and developed, it is necessary that diligent use be made of the exercise known as **Meditation or Mental Prayer.**

In Meditation divine truths are conveyed to the intellect; these are reflected upon, and studied in their relation and import to the soul; various affections toward God and acts of virtue spring from this study; and the soul is led to form practical resolutions for the avoiding of evil and the doing of good.

There are several so-called methods: the Ignatian, that of St. Sulpice, that of St. Francis de Sales and others. The one given in outline here is that of St. Francis de Sales.

According to this method Mental Prayer consists of three parts: **Preparation, Body and Conclusion,** each divided as indicated below.

### 1. PREPARATION.

1. **Remote,** consisting of purity of heart, i. e., freedom from sin; mortification of the passions, and habitual recollection.

2. **Less remote,** consisting in reading the principal points of the Meditation the previous evening, and trying to foresee the fruits and forecast the resolutions.

3. **Proximate,** consisting in making acts of faith, of the presence of God, adoration, contrition, humil-

ity, petition to God and the saints for grace to make the Meditation well. Then read the Meditation attentively. Attend to the representation of the subject as to place and other circumstances (also known as the Composition of Place).

## 2. BODY.

### 1. Considerations:

a) Try to define the subject; make an analysis of the words, texts and other passages.

b) Study the words, actions, sentiments of our Lord or the saints in relation to the subject.

c) Represent to yourself scenes from sacred history, the parables of our Lord, or such considerations as death, judgment, heaven, hell, etc.

d) Examine the various details by means of the following questions: Who? What? Where? By what means? How often? Why? How? When?

### 2. Affections, which together with Resolutions, are the most important part of the Meditation:

a) They are made by means of the so-called colloquies, i. e., conversations with God, our divine Saviour, the Blessed Virgin, the saints, the angels, etc.

b) They consist in various acts, such as of faith, hope, love, adoration, praise, thanksgiving, desire, regret, joy, sorrow, contrition, sympathy, reparation, trust, confidence, humility, self-abasement, surrender to God's holy will, zeal for His honor.

Note. As Meditation is to be a prayer and not a thinking exercise, care must be taken to make these affections the principal part of the exercise. The Considerations are necessary, but only as a means to an end. "We must think or reason so far as may be necessary, in order to set the heart or will in motion" (Bishop Hedley).

**3. Resolutions** (never to be omitted):

a) They should be few, but very definite and firm.

b) They should flow naturally from the subject; but it will be very useful to refer them to the subject of one's Particular Examen. (See next chapter.)

## 3. CONCLUSION.

**1. Thanksgiving** for the lights and graces received.

**2. Contrition** for distractions and negligences.

**3. Oblation** — offering oneself and the day's work to God.

**4. Petition**, begging for grace to spend the day well and carry out the resolutions.

**5. Spiritual Bouquet** — taking some text or maxim to be recalled at intervals during the day.

Observations:

As Meditation is naturally a difficult exercise, and as the devil does all in his power besides to make a soul neglect it, it is essential for progress in holiness and the love of God to be resolute and firm in making it faithfully every day. It must not be omitted because there seems to be no progress observable, or because distractions, or spiritual dryness or other difficulties are encountered. The very fact that a man makes an honest effort, and devotes the appointed time to it, means that he is making progress. His patient endurance of dryness and his efforts to struggle against distractions constitute in themselves a service that is very pleasing to God and very profitable to himself. True, it will not satisfy him; but precisely because of the difficulties encountered, it will be more meritorious than if he were favored with spiritual delights and consolations. The difficult prayer can be made the best prayer, as St. Francis de Sales teaches.

"With desolation is all the land made desolate because there is none that considereth in the heart" (Jer. 12:11).

# CHAPTER VII

## THE PARTICULAR EXAMEN

Another very necessary means of perfection is the exercise known as the Particular Examen, sometimes simply called the **Practice**.

### 1. NATURE OF THE PARTICULAR EXAMEN.

The Particular Examen differs from the General Examen in this, that it does not concern itself with all the sins and faults committed in the course of the day, but only with those committed against a particular virtue. It is restricted to one subject only; this may be the rooting out of a vice or bad habit, or the acquiring of some special virtue.

### 2. SOME GENERAL RULES.

1. To select a proper subject, confer with your confessor or guide of conscience, and let him assign it to you.

2. Study the subject as thoroughly as you can by consulting and reading about it.

3. It is a good thing to make a meditation on it now and then, say, once a week.

4. When making your morning offering, renew your particular resolution, and be sure to do so earnestly and prayerfully.

5. Try to foresee the occasions that may occur during the day for exercising yourself in your Prac-

tice. If it is a virtue, determine on a fixed number of acts, e. g., humility, the presence of God, confidence, etc.

6. If possible, let your daily meditation bear on your Practice, and form your resolutions in view of it.

## 3. METHOD OF MAKING IT.

1. At the time appointed, place yourself in the presence of God and pray earnestly for light to see and realize the faults you may have committed against your Practice.

2. Seriously and impartially examine into the faults you may have committed since your last Particular Examen, leaving all other sins and faults for the General Examen at night.

3. Make fervent acts of contrition for the faults discovered, or the acts of virtue omitted. Ask God's pardon and determine on some acts of penance. (These may consist in acts of self-denial or special prayers; the important thing is that some expiation be made.)

4. Make a firm resolution covering the period between this and your next Particular Examen.

## 4. VARIOUS HELPS.

1. To stimulate yourself to sustained fidelity, try to imagine that it is Jesus Christ Himself Who has assigned your Practice to you and asks you to work at it faithfully.

2. Foster a very fervent desire to make progress in it. Without this desire you will not make the necessary efforts.

3. Try to foresee what occasions may occur for exercising yourself in your Practice.

4. Now and then engage in an imaginary conflict, e. g., how you will remain silent under insults or reproof, or be patient when things go wrong, etc. (This may be done in regard to all the virtues except **Faith** and **Chastity.** The virtue of Chastity must never be made the subject of the Particular Examen.)

5. Rejoice when opportunities present themselves and brace yourself for the conflict.

6. If you succeed thank God for the victory; if you fail do not get discouraged, but make an act of sorrow, ask God's pardon and renew your resolution.

7. Never yield to discouragement, even if you fail repeatedly. Discouragement never comes from God and never leads to Him. It comes either from pride or from the devil.

8. Persevere faithfully, even if you perceive no progress. Progress is not always apparent. He who strives earnestly is making headway.

9. Do not change your Practice too often. Root out one fault before you attack another. Consult your confessor.

"If every year we rooted out one fault, we would soon become perfect" (*The Following of Christ*).

# CHAPTER VIII

# SELF-DENIAL, MORTIFICATION

In order that a seminarian may succeed in acquiring the perfection demanded of him by his vocation, he must learn to live by this rule laid down by Jesus Christ: "If anyone will come after Me, let him deny himself, take up his cross daily and follow Me." By self-denial he must seek to do penance for his past sins; keep from the commission of sins now and in the future; procure for himself the graces he needs for sanctifying himself in order to become a perfectly responsive instrument in the hands of God for the salvation of souls.

## 1. NATURE OF SELF-DENIAL.

1. **Scriptural terms:** Self-denial; self-abnegation; self-renunciation; renouncement; mortification; crucifixion of the flesh; the good fight; death and burial; stripping off the old man of sin and putting on the new man created according to Christ; dying to the world and to self and living to God.

2. **Modern terms:** Self-control; self-reformation; self-discipline; training of the will; cultivating will-power.

## 2. DEFINITIONS.

1. Struggling against our evil inclinations in order to subject them to the will, and the will to the law of God.

2. Obtaining the full control over our **passions,** so that these may help us to grow in grace and in the love of God.

### 3. THE PASSIONS.

1. The **passions (emotions)** are not something evil in themselves, for they are a necessary part of our nature, just as our five senses are. If placed permanently under the proper control of **reason** and **grace,** they become the means of great holiness and virtue, just as they become the source of much evil and sin if they are not brought under proper control.

2. Hence their proper training is absolutely necessary for growth in holiness. Their training can be compared to the training of a colt to make it a useful animal.

3. They are commonly divided into two groups: the so-called **Pleasure passions** and the **Aggressive passions** (also known as the **Concupiscible** and the **Irascible passions).**

4. The **Pleasure passions** are:

a) Love, and its opposite, Hatred.
b) Desire, and its opposite, Aversion.
c) Joy, and its opposite, Sadness.

5. The **Aggressive passions** are:

a) Courage, and its opposite, Fear.
b) Hope, and its opposite, Despair.
c) Anger, which has no opposite among the passions.

### 4. NECESSITY OF SELF-DENIAL.

1. **For salvation:**

a) For the avoidance of mortal sin.
b) For the avoidance of occasions of sin.

2. **For perfection:**

a) For the complete cancellation of the temporal punishment due to past sins.

b) For the imitation of Jesus Christ as demanded of every true follower of Christ.

c) For the practice of the perfection demanded of priests as ministers of Christ.

d) As a condition of success in the work of saving souls. "This kind [of devil] can go out by nothing but by prayer and fasting" (Mark 9:28).

## 5. GENERAL PRINCIPLES.

1. As to extension, self-denial embraces the whole man, both as to his body and as to his soul. Hence the division into exterior and interior mortification.

2. It demands the resolute abstention from all sinful and illicit pleasures.

3. It also demands abstention from many licit pleasures for the practice of penance and the training of the will in the doing of good.

4. For its proper practice the virtues of prudence and discretion are necessary. All excess must be avoided. The direction of one's confessor or spiritual adviser should be sought, and his advice should be followed faithfully.

## 6. SELF-DENIAL AS TO THE EXTERIOR SENSES.

1. Motives:

a) On account of original sin there is a life-long conflict between the spirit and the flesh. Our body is an ever-present enemy.

b) The glory of heaven is promised as a reward of self-denial. The members that suffer now will be glorified hereafter.

c) Fear of the pains of hell is a third motive. In case of perdition, the members that are pampered now shall suffer pain hereafter.

2. Means:

a) The observance of religious modesty at all times and in all places as to gait, posture, dress, etc., also when alone.

31

b) Faithful observance of the rules of Christian politeness and courtesy. This is also a means of practising the perfection of charity.

c) The eyes (windows of the soul): by practising custody, modesty and restraint, lest they see evil and suggestions to evil unnecessarily; avoiding theaters, movies, and all places where virtue is endangered.

d) The ears: by curbing one's curiosity and desire to hear news, gossip, detraction, calumny, etc.; limiting the use of the radio to what is useful or necessary.

e) The tongue: by observing silence and speaking but rarely; observing the rules of politeness as to conversation; refraining from all unkind remarks and speech, murmuring, fault-finding, criticism, etc.

f) The taste: by practising abstinence, moderation in eating and drinking; retrenching delicacies and little indulgences, leaving the best things to others, etc.

g) The sense of touch: by avoiding all softness and luxury in dress, furniture, and "creature-comforts" in general; patiently enduring heat and cold; carefully abstaining from all touches dangerous to chastity, either on oneself or others.

h) Daily duties: the faithful performance of these calls for the constant exercise of self-denial, e. g., promptness in rising, application to one's work and spiritual exercises, the fatigue caused by exertion, etc.

## 7. SELF-DENIAL AS TO THE INTERIOR SENSES.

1. Object:

a) The avoidance of dangerous fancies and recollections, and of what is known as "day-dreaming."

b) This applies also to the recalling of one's past sins of impurity. To examine into these, even for confession, is liable to prove dangerous.

c) The putting away of inordinate attachment to home, parents, relatives, friends, places and employments.

2. Means:

a) Whole-hearted application to the duties of one's state of life; discipline of the mind.

b) Healthful recreation to conserve one's health and strength to be able to do one's life-work; engaging in useful occupation.

c) Cultivating useful, noble and religious thoughts; also fostering holy desires (a very helpful means for keeping away evil thoughts and fancies, and banishing temptations).

## 8. DISCIPLINE OF THE INTELLECT.

1. Object and Means:

a) The overcoming of IGNORANCE, especially in matters of salvation and of the duties of one's state of life, by properly directed study and reading. (Spiritual reading.)

b) The overcoming of CURIOSITY, by avoiding unprofitable and dangerous study, reading, conversations and amusements.

c) The overcoming of PRIDE OF INTELLECT, by cultivating humility, docility, obedience, deference, reverence, etc.

d) The practice of "walking in the presence of God."

## 9. TRAINING OF THE WILL.

1. Obstacles to Be Removed:

a) Lack of reflection, which makes one act from impulse, caprice, passion, routine.

b) Over-eagerness and precipitancy.

c) Indifference, sloth, indecision.

d) Fear of failure, discouragement.

e) Human respect, fear of criticism, ridicule, persecution.

f) The bad example of others.

2. Means:

a) Cultivating a living faith, a deep conviction and a vivid realization of the truths of the Gospel.

b) Cultivating the qualities of decision and firmness.

c) Cultivating the qualities of constancy and perseverance.

"If any man will come after Me, let him deny himself, and take up his cross daily, and follow Me" (Luke 9:23).

"Whosoever doth not carry his cross and come after Me cannot be My disciple" (Luke 14:27).

"If you live according to the flesh, you shall die; but if by the Spirit you mortify the deeds of the flesh, you shall live" (Rom. 8:13).

"They that are Christ's have crucified their flesh with the vices and concupiscences" (Gal. 5:24).

"I chastise my body and bring it into subjection, lest perhaps when I have preached to others, I myself should become a castaway" (1 Cor. 9:27).

# CHAPTER IX

# THE VIRTUE OF HUMILITY

## 1. DEFINITION.

A supernatural virtue, which, through the self-knowledge it imparts, inclines us to consider ourselves at our true worth, and to seek self-effacement and contempt. "A virtue whereby a man, through a true knowledge of himself, becomes despicable in his own eyes" (St. Bernard).

## 2. WHAT IT IS NOT.

True humility does not consist in:

1. Shutting our eyes to the talents, ability, graces and accomplishments that we possess. These are God's gifts, for which we must be thankful, and which we must use for God's glory. (Example — the Blessed Virgin chanting the Magnificat.) To take the credit to ourselves would be contrary to humility.

2. Self-depreciation and self-criticism before others. This is often only a cloak for pride, or a means of soliciting praise from others, or an expression of discontent. True humility does not publish its faults, neither does it resent it when others draw attention to them.

3. Discouragement. This comes from wounded pride; we are more concerned about our own success than about the glory of God. It indicates a want of purity of intention and of resignation. True humility is willing to fail in its projects, if God so wills it.

### 3. WHAT HUMILITY IS.

True humility consists in the following three points:

1. **A full realization of** one's nothingness and sinfulness before almighty God. "A man becomes vile in his own eyes through a thorough knowledge of himself" (St. Bernard). We were born in sin; have committed many actual sins; are liable to commit very shameful sins in the future, and to be condemned. We are at best pardoned criminals; the stigma of sin is always upon us. What if our sins were made known to others?

2. **Willingness** to be despised and contemned according to our sinfulness. The conviction that we have deserved nothing less than hell for our sins makes us bear ridicule and contempt with patience and offer them up as a penance for our sins. A truly penitent soul courts humiliation and harbors no resentment against its authors.

3. **Giving glory to God alone** when we are successful in our undertakings. Success, instead of puffing us up, makes us recognize our helplessness and uselessness, and our unworthiness of the favors of God. We consider ourselves merely as the instruments which in His goodness He is pleased to make use of. (Compare: a pen in the hand of an author.)

### 4. SOME OF ITS EFFECTS.

The effects of humility are numerous. Here are a few:

1. **Patience and meekness,** in view of our sinfulness by which we deserve to suffer even eternal penalties.

2. **Confidence in God alone.** This excludes all presumptuous self-reliance.

3. **Charity and sympathy** for all around us, always esteeming others better than ourselves

4. **Compunction for our sins.** There are three degrees of sorrow for sin; attrition, contrition, compunction.

5. **Gratitude,** from a realization of God's infinite mercy and long-suffering.

6. **Ready obedience** to superiors. Obedience is an infallible test of true humility.

7. **Yielding** to the opinions of others in matters of indifference.

8. **Readiness** to seek counsel and help.

9. **Kindness,** gentleness and willingness to oblige.

10. **Observance** of the established rules of courtesy and politeness.

# CHAPTER X

## TEMPTATIONS

Since the proper evaluation of temptations and a correct knowledge of the manner in which we must meet them play a very important part in the spiritual life, we must give here an outline of this subject.

### 1. DEFINITIONS.

1. A Temptation is defined as a solicitation to evil on the part of our spiritual enemies: the world, the flesh, the devil.

2. Temptations of probation. These are more properly trials allowed or sent by God to the soul for the purpose of testing its virtue, and giving it opportunities of proving its love of Him. Such are: sickness, loss of the goods of fortune, false accusations, calumnies, etc.

3. Temptations of solicitation. These are suggestions or incitements to violation of the law of God, in thought, desire, word, action or omission of duty.

### 2. ELEMENTS OF TEMPTATION.

1. Presentation or suggestion, by which the attention of the mind is directed to evil, either by an internal act or by some external object or happening.

2. Delectation or pleasure, the feeling of delight or pleasure which accompanies the presentation and is inseparable from it. (Whenever the presentation

and the delectation are not wilful, they are not sinful, no matter how strong they may be.)

3. The action of the will, which manifests itself either in resistance and refusal, in which case there is no sin, but on the contrary, virtue; or in consent and compliance, in which case there is sin, either mortal or venial according to circumstances.

## 3. KINDS OF TEMPTATION.

1. Involuntary. These are suggestions to evil which come to us against our will and through no fault of ours; also such as come to us by reason of accidental or necessary exposure to what causes them. These are not sinful in themselves, no matter how vile they may be, or how long they may last.

2. Voluntary. These are suggestions to evil that we bring on ourselves by doing unnecessarily that which we know will give rise to them. These are sinful in themselves.

## 4. CAUSES OF TEMPTATIONS.

1. Original sin, which involved us in the loss of our integrity and the weakening of our natural faculties, and caused our being afflicted with the so-called "fomes peccati."

2. The devil, who either directly or indirectly suggests evil to us in order to lead us into sin, and through sin into hell.

3. The world, which abounds with all kinds of occasions of sin, such as: bad company, bad example, dangerous reading, dangerous amusements, false standards of morality.

4. The flesh, i. e., our fallen nature, which is continually craving for the enjoyment of sensual pleasure.

5. Our past sins, the remembrance of which (especially of sins of impurity) is often a troublesome source of new temptations.

6. Physical causes, such as irritations, inflammations or other ailments which commonly give rise to troublesome annoyances likely in turn to become the source of temptations against purity.

## 5. PURPOSE OF TEMPTATIONS.

1. Test of fidelity and sincerity in the service of God. They prove the soul and reveal its true character.

2. Means of atonement and penance. Resistance to them calls for the constant practice of self-denial and mortification.

3. Spiritual vigor and progress. The constant alertness necessary for victory keeps the soul from falling into lukewarmness and lethargy.

4. Growth in humility. Temptations teach the soul how weak and helpless it is, and how it must depend on the assistance of divine grace.

5. Growth in the love of God. One of the surest signs and best proofs of true love of God is the faithful keeping of His commandments.

6. Increase of grace and merit. Every victory over a temptation means growth in the virtue opposed to the temptation, and this in turn means increase in grace and merit for heaven.

## 6. CONDUCT DURING TEMPTATIONS.

1. We must always be vigilant so as never to expose ourselves to them without necessity. Unnecessary exposure invites disaster.

2. We must guard against presumption, especially if we have not been troubled with temptations for a long time.

3. At the same time we must not fear them too much. Exaggerated fear makes us think of them,

and thus makes it easier for them to take hold on us. It is good to cultivate a resoluteness and contempt for them.

4. We must pray often for the graces necessary to resist those that may come to us. This must be part of our daily devotion: "Lead us not into temptation."

5. When we are assailed we must resist them promptly, but not excitedly or nervously.

6. We must resist them energetically, not half-heartedly or weakly. But we must not resist them directly, but rather indirectly; i. e., after making a fervent aspiration for help, we must try to get interested in some other line of thought, without trying to wrestle, as it were, with the temptation.

7. We must resist perseveringly, not getting discouraged if the temptation continues to annoy us, or if it returns at frequent intervals.

8. We must seek to preserve calmness of soul, knowing that unwilful temptations, no matter how violent or persistent, are not sins.

9. It is advisable to make them known to our confessor, not as a matter of accusation, but for the purpose of obtaining advice. Such a manifestation is an act of humility, which often gets its immediate reward in the form of deliverance from the temptation.

Note. In this connection it is helpful to consider the examples of the saints, such as St. Catherine of Siena, who was assured by our divine Lord that He was in her soul while she was undergoing violent temptations against holy purity; of St. Mary Magdalen de Pazzis, who for over four years endured severe temptations against different virtues; of St. Mary of Egypt, who was subjected to very trying temptations for seventeen years — the same length of time that she had before spent in sin; and St. Vincent de Paul, who for several years endured very painful temptations against the virtue of faith.

# CHAPTER XI

## SENSIBLE DEVOTION

As there are many who have erroneous ideas about the character of true devotion and true service of God, we must now explain four important subjects that are closely connected with this topic. They are: Sensible Devotion, Lukewarmness, Spiritual Dryness and True Devotion.

### 1. NATURE OF SENSIBLE DEVOTION.

Sensible Devotion (or sensible consolations) consists in certain tender emotions that affect our sensibility and cause us to experience feelings of spiritual joy. They affect the body, accelerate the heartbeat, quicken the circulation, alter the expression of the features, cause tears to flow, and the like.

### 2. SOURCES.

The sources of this kind of devotion are threefold:

1. **God.** God at times grants it to the soul especially in the beginning of its consecration to His service, in order to attract and encourage it to perseverance. Therein God acts like a gardener who carefully waters a newly planted fruit-tree until he is assured that it has taken root in the soil.

2. **The devil.** But it may also be caused by the devil who acts on the imagination, the feelings and the nervous system of a person in order to lead him astray, either by inducing him to undertake dangerous austerities which will undermine his health or

lead to discouragement; or by trying to foster in him sentiments of pride, vanity, presumption, etc.

3. Nature. Lastly, it may be due to one's natural temperament or condition of health, or to such accidental things as food, climate, the condition of the atmosphere, etc. These causes affect both body and soul very intimately, and may promote Sensible Devotion on the one hand or Dryness on the other.

### 3. ADVANTAGES.

1. That Sensible Devotion which comes from God facilitates the knowledge and love of Him, so that the soul becomes eager to acquire greater knowledge of divine things and to serve God with greater earnestness.

2. It helps to strengthen the will to perform the more difficult things of the spiritual life, to resist temptations and to suffer patiently in times of trial and persecution.

3. It also helps in forming habits of recollection and of union with God.

### 4. DANGERS.

But Sensible Devotion — even that which comes from God — carries with it certain serious dangers: These are:

1. Spiritual greed or gluttony, through which one "seeks the consolations of God, and not the God of consolations," as St. Francis de Sales puts it. It easily leads to the neglect of duty and the refusal to make the sacrifices necessary in the service of God.

2. Self-complacency, by which one imagines himself to stand high in the grace and friendship of God.

3. Vanity, which tempts one to make his spiritual favors known to others and to desire to be thought much of on account of them.

**4. Presumption,** by which one thinks himself strong and invincible in time of temptation, and hence is apt to expose himself rashly to temptations and occasions of sin.

## 5. ATTITUDE TO BE MAINTAINED.

1. We may desire Sensible Devotion **conditionally,** that is, if it is for the good of our soul.

2. We must receive it with gratitude and humility.

3. We must **not enjoy it for its own sake,** but employ it according to God's purpose.

4. We must be **willing to do without it** and be determined to serve God with perfect fidelity even if it is withdrawn.

Note. From the foregoing explanation it is plain that Sensible Devotion — feelings of devotion, emotional piety and the like — is not at all necessary for true devotion. Sometimes it is a hindrance rather than a help to the perfect love and service of God. This is the case when a person serves God more on account of the consolations he experiences than out of pure love.

# CHAPTER XII

## LUKEWARMNESS

Lukewarmness is a very dangerous spiritual disease which may attack beginners or even perfect souls. Unless it is cured, it invariably does great harm to the soul. Hence every care must be taken to guard against it.

### 1. NATURE OF LUKEWARMNESS.

Lukewarmness consists in a sort of spiritual languor which saps the energies of the will, inspires horror for effort, and thus leads to a decline of the Christian life.

### 2. CAUSES OF LUKEWARMNESS.

1. Defective nourishment of the soul either by the **omission of spiritual exercises,** such as meditation, spiritual reading, prayer, examination of conscience, the practice of virtue, the duties of one's state of life; or by the **negligent performance** of them, by slovenliness, lack of purity of intention, etc.

2. This neglect, or careless performance, of one's spiritual exercises naturally produces a gradual weakening of the soul, which easily becomes a prey to various vices, such as pride, vanity, sensuality, envy, discontent, moroseness, etc. These in turn become the source of countless venial sins.

### 3. DANGERS OF LUKEWARMNESS.

1. **Spiritual blindness.** As when the eyesight becomes impaired a man is not able to see things

clearly, so the conscience of a lukewarm person cannot see the sinfulness of sin. The judgment becomes warped, and often serious sins are considered as slight ones.

**2. Weakening of the will.** By dint of making concessions to sensuality and to pride in small things, the will to resist temptations is gradually weakened, so that a lapse into serious sin is only a matter of time. In the meantime venial sins keep on growing in number; and grace is being constantly abused.

**3. Difficulty of cure.** The condition of a lukewarm soul is very much like the condition of a person suffering from tuberculosis. The cure of this is difficult, especially in advanced stages; frequently it is altogether impossible. So too is the cure of lukewarmness extremely difficult. It requires great will power for a lukewarm person to abandon his easygoing ways and lead a life of regularity.

## 4. LUKEWARMNESS DIFFERS FROM DRYNESS.

Uninstructed persons often mistake Lukewarmness for Dryness. The difference is very great. Lukewarmness is a state of the will, Dryness a state of the feelings. Lukewarmness is sinful, because it is voluntary — wilful; Dryness is not sinful, because it is involuntary — unwilful.

Lukewarmness is productive of countless infidelities in the service of God and of many venial sins; but Dryness, when properly dealt with, becomes the occasion of perfect and even heroic service of God, and therefore of great increase in grace here and eternal glory hereafter. (See next chapter.)

## 5. SIGNS OF LUKEWARMNESS.

Lukewarmness can easily be recognized by the following signs.

**1. Facility in omitting exercises of piety.** This is the direct contradictory of true fervor.

**2. Negligence** in those exercises which we perform. They are full of venial sins.

**3. Neglect of proper self-examination.** Confessions and Communions are mere routine affairs. There is no improvement after Confession, no fruits of Holy Communion.

4. Habitual acting without purity of intention.

**5. Carelessness** in forming habits of virtue, lack of effort to profit by given opportunities.

**6. Contempt of little things**, hence neglect and slovenly performance of them, e. g., Sign of the Cross, genuflections, prayers.

**7. Vain complacency;** thinking rather of the good we have done than the good we have left undone; comparing ourselves with those whom we consider less perfect.

## 6. DISTRACTIONS IN PRAYER.

In this connection a few words about distractions in prayer are necessary.

**1. Voluntary distractions.** Those which we entertain knowingly, freely and wilfully, or for the repression of which we make but feeble efforts; those which spring from causes which we do not avoid or suppress. Voluntary distractions are always sinful and hence constitute a distinct spiritual loss.

**2. Involuntary distractions.** Those which we earnestly strive to overcome, or reduce in number. These are not sinful; on the contrary, the efforts made to dispel them and to be recollected become a part of our service of God. Perseverance in prayer in spite of such distractions is very necessary for progress in the spiritual life.

# CHAPTER XIII

## SPIRITUAL DRYNESS

A difficulty very often encountered in the spiritual life consists in what is known as **Spiritual Dryness or Aridity.** A correct understanding of this subject and of the manner in which it must be dealt with is very necessary, else there is a danger that a person will fail in fidelity and perseverance when subjected to this trial.

### 1. NATURE OF SPIRITUAL DRYNESS.

1. Spiritual Dryness consists in a privation of those sensible and spiritual consolations which make the exercise of prayer and the practice of virtue easy.

2. It manifests itself in several ways and in various degrees of intensity: want of relish in prayer and other spiritual exercises, the feeling of irksomeness and distaste for them; weariness and torpor of soul; aversion, sometimes even positive disgust and repugnance, for the service of God in its entire range; finally, a state of darkness and desolation in which the soul shares to some extent the dereliction which our divine Saviour experienced during His agony in Gethsemane and on the Cross. At such times the soul can apply itself to its accustomed spiritual exercises only by sheer force of will.

3. Again, as stated above, Dryness or Aridity must not be confounded with Lukewarmness or Tepidity. The difference is mainly this: Dryness is a matter of the feelings (absence of sensible devotion);

whereas Lukewarmness is a matter of the will (wilful negligence in the service of God). Lukewarmness is therefore a sinful state, because it is wilful; while Dryness, not being wilful, is not sinful. On the very contrary, it is meant to be a means of perfect love of God and of great growth in grace and merit.

## 2. PURPOSE OF SPIRITUAL DRYNESS.

1. **Detachment from self and from creatures.** The soul is to learn to abandon self and to seek God alone, and serve Him faithfully for His own sake.

2. **Humility.** The soul is to learn that consolations are not our right, but a free gift of God which He often withholds in punishment of our infidelities or to test our virtue.

3. **Purification of the soul.** The soul is expected to convert the keen sufferings which result from the various forms of dryness into means of expiation of sins, atonement and penance.

4. **Grounding in solid virtue.** That the soul may remain faithful in times of dryness, it must have constant recourse to fervent prayer and must seek to develop great power of will.

5. Occasions of **rapid growth in perfect love of God,** Who is to be loved and served with a love that is free from self-interest.

6. Occasions of **gaining vast treasures of grace and merit** which could be gained in no other way.

In general it is to be remembered that it is not the easy things of our service that enable us to practise the most perfect love of God, but the things that are difficult and tax the strength and power of our soul.

# CHAPTER XIV

## TRUE DEVOTION

Lastly, it is of greatest importance that a seminarian acquire a correct knowledge of what constitutes true devotion, i. e., the kind of devotion which will enable him to persevere steadfastly in the pursuit of the virtue and holiness demanded of him by his holy vocation.

**1. WHAT TRUE DEVOTION IS NOT.**

1. **It does not consist in exaltation of the feelings and imagination.** Feelings are very deceptive and misleading in the spiritual life.

2. **Nor in vehemence of emotions.** Emotions are commonly traceable to temperament; they come and go; their presence depending largely on physical causes.

3. **Nor in a multiplicity of devotions.** Some persons burden themselves with a large number of pious exercises, with the result that they perform them badly and often neglect the more important duties of their state of life.

4. **Nor in austerities,** such as fasting, inflicting pain on oneself, and the like, especially when these are undertaken without the direction and permission of the guide of one's conscience.

5. **Nor in spiritual consolations,** since — as was explained above — these are either God's gift to us, or they may be purely natural, or may even be caused by the devil.

6. **Nor in mere external activity.** This is not rarely found to co-exist with neglect or wretched perform-

ance of prayer, and with lack of purity of intention. It may be merely an expression of a restlessness of temperament, or be prompted by the desire of human applause.

7. **Nor in ecstasies, revelations, visions, etc.**; nor even in the gift of miracles. If these are genuine they are simply God's gifts to the soul, and not the soul's gift to God. Usually they are the reward of long-continued and faithful service.

## 2. WHAT TRUE DEVOTION IS.

True devotion consists essentially in three things which are within reach of every man of good-will.

1. **Perfect fidelity to every duty** as it comes along, as to both time and other circumstances. There is no wilful neglect or omission of any known duty, not even the smallest. This fidelity is maintained perseveringly at all times, but especially in periods of dryness or want of consolation, even though these be of long standing. "He that hath [knows] My commandments and keepeth them, he it is that loveth Me."

2. **Completeness of every action.** There is no haste or hurry to get through with one's duty; no slovenly performance, no skimping, no acting on the "good enough" principle; but every action is performed as perfectly as possible, as though it were the last action of one's life. The soul acts on the principle that "there are no trifles in the service of God."

3. **Purity of intention.** Every action is performed, not from motives of selfishness or expediency, or human applause, but solely for the greater honor and glory of God. It is intended to be an expression of perfect love of Him. "If you love Me, keep My commandments." This purity of intention is a matter of the will, and not of the feelings; hence it can always be made, and with great fervor too, even in times of darkest desolation of spirit. At such times the soul is still able to say with fullest earnestness: "My dearest Jesus, this is for love of You." "Father, not my will but Thine be done."

# CHAPTER XV

## PERSONAL LOVE OF JESUS CHRIST

In order that a seminarian may apply himself perseveringly to the naturally hard and distasteful work of striving after the perfection required by his sublime vocation, he must labor earnestly at fostering an ardent and intense personal love for his divine Master Jesus Christ. For this purpose he must meditate much on the assurances which our Lord gives to His priests that He loves them as His Father loves Him; that He calls them, and wishes them to be, His friends; and that He pleads for a return of love in these words: "Abide in My love."

### 1. MOTIVES FOR FOSTERING AN ARDENT PERSONAL LOVE.

1. **His Person.** In Him are found supreme beauty, goodness and love. His life and character are the most sublime. The splendor of His glorified humanity will be the source of ecstatic joy to the blessed in heaven.

2. **His words.** In these we possess the one saving and life-giving doctrine; also most gracious and generous promises of endless glory hereafter. What would our life be without these?

3. **His works.** These are all manifestations of infinite compassion and mercy. Our redemption through His bitter Passion and Death proves that He loved us more than His own life.

**4. His gifts.** These are most wonderful in every way: sanctifying and actual grace; the Sonship of God; the right to heaven; the sacraments, especially the Blessed Eucharist; the PRIESTLY VOCATION; and the life of glory hereafter.

## 2. KINDS OF LOVE TO BE PRACTISED TOWARD HIM.

**1. Love of complacency.** This kind of love is practised by frequent meditation on His life and actions on earth and His glory in heaven; on His majesty, power and happiness; and on His glorified humanity. Also by rejoicing at the worship, honor and glory He receives from the whole creation, but especially from the Church, and the angels and saints in heaven. This love prompts the soul to make many fervent acts of adoration, praise and thanksgiving. "Laudamus te, benedicimus te, adoramus te, glorificamus te. Gratias agimus tibi propter magnam gloriam tuam."

**2. Love of benevolence.** This is practised by fostering the ardent desire to see Him loved and honored by all His creatures; by cultivating a burning zeal for the promotion of the knowledge and love of Him through fervent prayer, instructing and catechizing the ignorant, spreading good reading matter, helping the missions, etc. It prompts souls to pray and suffer for the conversion of sinners; to make reparation and atonement for the many sins and insults offered to God the world over; and especially to offer themselves to God to be victims of expiation for the sins of others.

**3. Love of esteem.** This love is practised by the cultivation of a profound reverence for His sacred Person and for everything that relates to Him in any way, such as blessed and consecrated objects, sacred places, the Sacred Scriptures; as also for every neighbor as His representative and the purchase of His most precious Blood, especially those persons

53

that are consecrated to Him by vows or Holy Orders. It manifests itself by the reverent and devout performance of prayer, and particularly by a sustained effort to carry out faithfully all the ceremonies prescribed for sacred functions.

4. **Love of friendship.** This kind of love is practised by cultivating union of mind, heart and sentiment. The proof of true friendship is found in living according to the rule: "Idem velle, idem nolle, ea demum firma amicitia est." He who seeks to practise this love will foster a great delicacy of conscience (not scrupulosity) in regard to everything sinful; he will never do what he knows to be displeasing to our Lord, and will be ready to do always and generously whatever he recognizes to be his Master's will. He will gladly make sacrifices for the love of Him, and generously suffer inconveniences and persecution for His sake. "I will not now call you servants; ... but I have called you friends."

5. **Love of desire.** This is cultivated by fostering an ardent longing and desire "to be dissolved and to be with Christ," in order to enjoy the unspeakable bliss of the Beatific Vision and be confirmed in His grace and love; yet being willing to live long and being grateful for every moment added to this earthly life, since every such moment can be made the means of much growth in grace here and of a corresponding increase of eternal glory hereafter. One who has this love is willing to live long in order to do as much as possible for the promotion of God's glory and the salvation of souls.

### 3. MEANS OF CULTIVATING THESE KINDS OF LOVE.

1. He who would practise these five kinds of love must first of all retire as much as possible from the many distractions entailed by unnecessary contact with the world and its spirit.

2. There must be meditation and reflection on the life, words and example of Jesus Christ.

3. Care must be taken to avoid all deliberate sins and imperfections as being the direct opposite of true love, and to expiate promptly whatever sins may be committed.

4. Finally, there must be the practice of making frequent visits to the Blessed Sacrament; of making a pious use of pictures, the crucifix and other devotional articles.

"As the Father hath loved Me, I have loved you. Abide in My love.... I will not now call you servants; ... but I have called you friends.... You are My friends, if you do the things that I command you.... He that hath My commandments, and keepeth them, he it is that loveth Me.... If you love Me, keep My commandments."

## CHAPTER XVI

## THE CHARACTERISTICS OF THE PERFECT

The characteristics of those who, whether in the world or in the cloister, have cultivated the higher perfection and have advanced some way in its attainment, are the following:

1. They take a true view of themselves, not distorted by blindness or conceit, and this view is a lowly one.

2. They take a true view of life, remembering that this world passes away, that the next is eternal, and that man's great duty is to glorify God and to save his own soul.

3. They have a horror of sin above all other evils; they avoid every occasion that may lead them into it; and if unfortunately they fall at times through surprise or human weakness, they hasten to do penance and reconcile themselves with God.

4. They shun the world and the spirit of worldliness; they despise its highest interests; disregard its opinions; and will not conform to its ways of laxity and vice.

5. In all things they trace the hand of divine Providence and adore God's wonderful ways; they conform themselves to His disposal of things, and trust themselves with confidence to His guidance.

6. They esteem and love God and delight in Him beyond all else; they taste His sweetness, and repose in Him.

**7. They listen to God's inspirations;** they endeavor to advance His glory; promote the knowledge and service of Him by others; and work always with Him and for Him.

**8. They have a personal love for our Lord Jesus Christ;** they live in constant union with Him; and they love and serve all mankind as His brethren and as the purchase of His most precious Blood.

Consider each of these points separately and endeavor to regulate your actions accordingly.

# CHAPTER XVII

## SUPERNATURAL MERIT

### 1. OUR DESTINY: ETERNAL GLORY IN HEAVEN.

1. **Our destiny is supernatural.** In Baptism we were made adopted children of God, co-heirs with Jesus Christ and true heirs of the eternal glory of heaven.

2. **Our title to heaven is inalienable;** it cannot be taken from us. But we can lose it, and actually do lose it, by the commission of mortal sin.

3. **The glory of heaven consists in the sight, possession and perfect love of God** (enjoyment of God) for all eternity.

4. **A particular degree of this glory will be awarded to everyone who dies in the state of sanctifying grace.**

5. **This particular degree** is determined in each case **by the kind and number of supernatural merits a** person has acquired during life. Every man is rewarded according to his works.

6. **Our duty in this life is to love and serve God** with our whole heart, whole soul, whole mind and whole strength, and our neighbor as ourselves, and thereby qualify for the possession of the glory of heaven. The perfect fulfillment of this duty demands the performance of all kinds of good works, i. e., meritorious works.

### 2. KINDS OF MERIT.

1. **Merit in general.** What a man earns for himself by work done according to prescribed conditions.

2. **Natural merit.** Temporal reward earned by good works performed by a person not in the state of sanctifying grace; i. e., by a person in the state of original or of mortal sin.

3. **Supernatural merit.** Heavenly and eternal reward earned by good works performed by a person in the state of sanctifying grace.

4. **Condign merit.** Reward due on account of having fulfilled the conditions of a contract or agreement. Heavenly glory is the reward of condign merit. (See No. 4, 3.)

5. **Congruous merit.** Reward given over and above that which was agreed upon. (Like a bonus to a faithful servant.)

## 3. MEANS OF MERIT.

1. **Sanctifying grace.** The soul must be in supernatural union with God, free from original and mortal sin.

2. **Actual or helping grace.** The grace that is a necessary aid in the performance of supernatural good works.

3. **Co-operation with actual grace.** God supplies the grace, but we must co-operate with it as prescribed. God's grace and our will must work together. Without this there is no merit.

4. **Good works.** By this we understand every good thought, word and act that is done for the glory of God. Every human action that is not sinful can be made meritorious for heaven. Hence all good thoughts, kind words, acts of charity, aspirations, prayers, the performance of the duties of one's state of life, the patient endurance of sufferings, can be made meritorious; as also even the so-called indifferent actions, as eating, drinking, rest, recreation, etc., when done for the glory of God.

## 4. CONDITIONS OF MERIT.

1. **General condition.** The acquiring of supernatural merit is restricted to man's life on earth, and ceases at the moment of death.

2. We acquire merit only by reason of the infinite merits of Jesus Christ. Hence union with Him by grace is necessary.

3. **God has bound Himself by promise** to give an eternal reward for our supernaturally good works. Were it not for this promise, we could claim no reward hereafter.

4. **The state of sanctifying grace.** Without this it is impossible to merit supernaturally. Good works done in the state of original or of mortal sin merit only a natural reward, such as good health, prosperity, success in undertakings, etc.

5. **Supernatural intention,** by which our good works are done for the love and glory of God, and not from selfish motives.

## 5. REWARDS MERITED.

1. **Increase of sanctifying grace.** Each and every good work adds to the amount of grace possessed. (May be illustrated by the growth of knowledge.)

2. **Remission of temporal punishment of sin.** Every meritorious work helps to cancel this punishment.

3. **Impetration or Intercession.** Every meritorious work has the power of prayer before God.

4. **Actual graces.** These are obtained by reason of congruous merit.

5. **Increase of glory in heaven.** Every good action entitles us to a corresponding reward in heaven. The measure of glory allotted to each of the blessed corresponds to the sum of all the merits he possessed at the time of his death.

## 6. CAUSES OF DIFFERENCE OF MERIT.

**1. The particular degree of sanctifying grace** with which the good work is done. The higher this degree, the more meritorious the work. As grace increases, the same good work becomes more meritorious each time it is performed. (Illustrated by the increase of interest in the case of compound interest.)

**2. The intrinsic excellency of good works.** Good works differ greatly in value. Some, such as the Holy Mass and Holy Communion, are vastly more excellent than others.

**3. The degree of purity of intention.** A very pure intention gives great value to even very small actions.

**4. The frequent renewal of the good intention.** This intensifies the will and promotes purity of intention.

**5. The number of good works.** This is self-evident.

**6. The difficulties encountered.** As a rule, the more difficult a good work is, the more meritorious it can be made.

**7. The particular state of life.** Other things being equal, the state of Virginity is more meritorious than that of Matrimony, and the state of Religion than that of Virginity.

"Carefully study to present thyself approved unto God, a workman that needeth not to be ashamed, rightly handling the word of truth" (2 Tim. 2:15).

"Meditate upon these things, be wholly in these things: that thy profiting may be manifest to all. Take heed to thyself and to doctrine; be earnest in them. For in doing this, thou shalt both save thyself and them that hear thee" (1 Tim. 4:15, 16).

"Godliness is profitable to all things, having promise of the life that now is, and that which is to come" (1 Tim. 4:8).

61

# APPENDIX

## OBLIGATION TO HOLINESS

### Thoughts for Seminarians

*A Sublime Destiny.*

1. The marvelous grace of vocation to the sacred priesthood has been granted to you by the infinite love and goodness of God. It is a grace that greatly surpasses all other graces that God bestows on men in the present order of things. Just as the Divine Maternity is the most sublime dignity that could be conferred on a creature, so the grace of priestly vocation is the greatest grace that can be bestowed on a Catholic young man. It is your destiny to be elevated in grace and power high above the angelic orders. The Cherubim and Seraphim, despite their flaming love of God and near approach to His throne, are not empowered to offer up the tremendous Sacrifice of the Mass nor to absolve repentant sinners, as is given to the humblest priest to do as a regular, life-long function. And this sublime vocation is yours.

*Obligation of Holiness*

2. Quite naturally so sublime a vocation imposes on you the strict obligation of acquiring a very high degree of holiness. It should be the highest that is attainable by a human being. The combination of the spotless purity of an angel and of the great sanctity of St. John the Baptist would not be too great; strictly speaking, it would not be great enough. But the attainment of this is out of all

question for you. Nor does God require it of you. What He does require, however, is that particular degree of holiness which is in proportion to the measure of special vocational graces He has allotted to you by reason of the vocation He has given you. Of this truth you must have a keen realization.

### Think Well on It.

3. Several very important points there are with which you must make yourself perfectly familiar at the very outset of your seminary career. Much thought and reflection must be given to them. First, in His infinite love and goodness God has called you to the sublimest dignity and office in the kingdom of His Church, namely to be "another Christ"; second, this calling imposes on you the strict duty of laboring strenuously to acquire a holiness commensurate with it; third, in view of your calling, God has apportioned to you a large fund of special graces designed to enable you to reach the degree of holiness demanded of you; fourth, you must generously respond to God's loving designs on you, and resolutely giving up whatever stands in the way, apply your whole energy to the task of acquiring that holiness, that you may become a perfectly responsive instrument in the hands of God for the promotion of His glory and the salvation of immortal souls.

### Two Requisites.

4. Further, you must have a full conviction that your success in this important undertaking depends on two indispensable means, namely the *grace of God* and *your own good-will*, as expressed by a faithful and unwavering co-operation with that grace. There must be a harmonious working together of divine grace and your good-will for the obtaining of the desired results. The one without

the other is useless. Even the most powerful of God's graces will remain wholly fruitless if there is no faithful co-operation of will on your part; and no matter how strong and vigorous your will may be by nature, it is utterly powerless to advance a single step in the way of priestly holiness if the help of God's grace be wanting to you.

### An Illustration.

5. We have a very instructive illustration of this important truth in the working of the steam engine. That it may do work, two things are essential: a perfectly adjusted mechanism, and a sufficient pressure of steam. The engine alone cannot produce results, no matter how accurately its parts are constructed; neither can the steam alone, no matter how tremendous its pressure. So too, the engine cannot do work if any parts are bent or broken or rusted, though the pressure of steam is high; nor though the parts are in good order, if the required pressure is lacking. The comparison is not perfect; but it is complete enough to let you see how essential is the proper interrelation between the grace of God and the co-operation which you must contribute with your free will.

### Not Given Gratis.

6. A full realization of your strict duty to apply yourself diligently to the acquisition of a high degree of sacerdotal sanctity is therefore a necessary prerequisite for success. So too is the realization of your obligation to co-operate faithfully with the graces God has so liberally set aside for you. Guard against harboring the fatal delusion that somehow holiness will grow of itself and without painstaking efforts on your part; or that it will be given to you by God gratis and as a finished article; or that it will be bestowed on you in perfection on the day of your

ordination to the priesthood. You might just as wisely expect the necessary knowledge of sacerdotal science to be infused into your mind by a miracle, or bestowed on you in the reception of sacred orders. Both sanctity and learning must be acquired by proper painstaking efforts. Sanctity especially is not given freely to anyone, least of all to one who has no earnest desire for it. "The kingdom of heaven suffers violence."

## Natural Repugnance.

7. Let us right here point out two very serious obstacles that you must be prepared to struggle against as long as you live. The first is the *natural dislike* you experience for the painful efforts necessary to avoid sin, to subdue your passions, to root out evil habits and to practise virtue. Nature, tainted and weakened by sin, abhors the labor required for a holy life. It hates self-denial and craves self-indulgence. And thus the striving after holiness is very much like the labor involved in rowing upstream in a swiftly flowing current. You make progress only when and as long as you ply the oars. The very moment you stop to take a rest, you are carried downstream, even though you may be only a few feet from your destination. And if you rest long enough, you will be carried far beyond the point of your departure. A graphic picture, this, of what goes on in the spiritual life. To make progress and reach your destination, you must labor hard, incessantly and perseveringly to the very end.

## The Devil's Enmity.

8. The second obstacle is the *enmity of Satan*. Satan knows full well what a mighty power for good a holy priest is; how much such a one will contribute to the destruction of his empire, and how many souls he will snatch from hell and send on their way to heaven. Quite

naturally then, this enemy of God and man will do all in his power to render the priest's labor as difficult as possible. He will do all he can to make good priests fall from grace, and to hinder the proper development of those who are preparing for sacred orders. He will insinuate low views of the sanctity required by the priestly state; will magnify and multiply temptations of all kinds; will try to put bad example in their way, and even prepare persecutions for them in the hope of making them fall, or at least of crippling their efficiency for good. To have succeeded in making a seminarian lead a careless and tepid life and thus to reduce his future efficiency by ten, or twenty, or forty percent, will mean the loss of many souls. And what a wild shout of triumph rings through the dungeons of hell when the devil has succeeded also in dragging the shepherd into the infernal abyss! No wonder he is tireless in his activities in seminaries to make low ideals the accepted standards. "Satan hath desired to have you" is true of every seminarian.

### *Your Responsibility.*

9. This much is therefore certain beyond room for dispute: God demands of you a high degree of holiness, and He has allotted to you all the graces you need for this purpose. He has also placed you under strict obligation to "trade with your talents," that is, to make the best possible use of your graces. In the hour of your judgment after death He will exact a most rigorous account of every grace you have received in your life, as also of the fruits of virtue that you should have acquired by a faithful co-operation. What answer will you give and what excuse will you advance if you are found deficient in the holiness required of you by reason of your priestly vocation?

*God's Standards.*

10. It is very helpful in stimulating to fervor to remember that in this judgment you will not be examined according to the low standards of conduct that your sin-inclined and pleasure-loving nature may have prompted you to adopt; nor according to the low ideals which may have prevailed among your fellow-seminarians and which you may have accepted as your own in order to escape the harsh criticism and derision to which the pursuit of high ideals would have exposed you. You did not have the courage to be different from the crowd. As if faithful imitation of Christ did not make it necessary to be different! No, you will be judged impartially and rigorously according to the perfectly just, unerring and unchanging standards set up by Jesus Christ, Whose representative and minister you are called to be.

*War on Venial Sin.*

11. In the next place you must know that there are two elementary requisites for progress in holiness. The first is the *firm determination and persevering effort to avoid to the best of your ability all deliberate venial sins.* Since holiness is in the last analysis nothing else than the perfect love of God, it stands to reason that one who has this love in his heart cannot go on knowingly and wilfully doing what is insulting and offensive to Him, no matter how small and trifling the wrong may appear to be. Fire and water could not be more opposed to each other than are the perfect love of God and deliberate venial sin. They are antagonistic and irreconcilable. He who maintains that he loves God with his whole heart, soul, mind and strength, yet does not hesitate to commit "little" sins, either is a liar or has an altogether wrong view of the nature of sanctity.

67

*Danger of Lax Views.*

12. A very common obstacle to progress in holiness that many seminarians encounter is the pernicious evil of fostering lax views of venial sin. Often they learn in moral theology to their great surprise that many actions which they had always considered to be mortally sinful are said to be only venially so; and this newly acquired knowledge becomes for some a great temptation henceforth to indulge in these actions without fear and remorse. Thus they come to make light of venial sin and to trifle with it. Instead of cultivating a growing hatred of it and fostering a delicacy of conscience in regard to it, as one will do who aspires to the perfect love of God, they daringly take the liberty to offend and insult God without hesitation, not considering the malice of their action nor the great harm they inflict on their own souls. "Oh, it is only a venial sin; it doesn't amount to much; it doesn't even need to be confessed" is not rarely adopted as the norm of conduct by those who are by their vocation obliged to aim at the very highest degrees of Christian perfection.

*Little Sins?*

13. There is in most people a strong inclination to take lax views of venial sin because it naturally falls in with their inborn aversion for the efforts necessary to avoid such sins, and with the persistent cravings they experience to indulge in certain liberties and pleasures which cannot be enjoyed without staining the soul with sin of some kind or other. This strong craving for sensual pleasure makes people invent all kinds of excuses and arguments with which they try to justify the commission of what they choose to call "little" sins. This is bound to occur in those who have not learned the absolute necessity of self-denial and mortification, by which the unruly desires of sin-tainted nature must be held in check, and

the flesh subjected to the spirit, and the spirit to the law of God.

*Inviting Disaster.*

14. From this it follows that the seminarian who does not strive to cultivate a great delicacy and sensitiveness of conscience (not scrupulosity, let it be understood) in regard to deliberate venial sin, and who does not take pains to avoid it to the best of his ability, but makes light of it and commits it unhesitatingly, is heading for spiritual disaster. He who knows the workings of the human heart perfectly assures us: "He that is unjust in that which is little will also be unjust in that which is greater." He who freely commits venial sins, be it for the sake of comfort, or from human respect, or from some friendship, or from a dread and fear of self-denial, or for the sake of some passing pleasure, or to get out of some difficulty, is seriously neglecting the work of his sanctification. Unless he reforms and changes his tactics, he will never acquire the holiness demanded of him by his vocation. He is guilty of a deliberate abuse of grace which, unless he repents and amends, will lead him head-long into great spiritual ruin. Unfaithfulness in little things is a presage to unfaithfulness in greater ones. It is folly to question God's pronouncement on this head.

*Abuse of Grace.*

15. Closely allied to venial sin, in fact inseparable from it, is the evil of *abuse of grace.* After venial sin, learn to fear nothing more than what goes by the name of abuse, or bad use of, God's grace. Never forget that every grace that you receive has been purchased for you with the Blood of Jesus Christ, and is therefore an infinitely precious gift of God. Every grace properly used means that you are practising virtue and therefore acquiring an

eternal reward for yourself. In addition to this you receive additional graces to enable you to do more good and to make a steady advance in holiness. But every grace abused, or used badly, or not at all, will be tantamount to a slighting of God's best gift, and will earn for you a just punishment, besides breaking the continuity of the chain of certain graces that God had destined for you as being necessary for the success of some future work.

### Practice of Virtue.

16. After the avoidance of venial sin, the second elementary requisite for progress in holiness is the *constant, resolute and wholehearted endeavor* to practise the various virtues that go to make up the perfection of a follower of Christ, and especially of one who is called to the sublime dignity of the priestly state. To be able to do this successfully you will do well to begin by mastering the great secret of cultivating a lively sense of the presence of God, and especially of walking in spirit with your divine Saviour, as the Apostles during the three years of the training were privileged to walk with Him in body. You must master the important art of keeping Him in your mind and before your eyes in such a way that you never quite lose sight of Him during the day, even in your busiest moments, but often think of Him as easily and as naturally as the magnetic needle turns toward the pole.

### Personal Love of Christ.

17. In other words, you must foster and develop in your soul a very ardent personal love of Jesus Christ. You must not regard Him as a mere abstraction, nor as a mere historical personage, nor as a person far removed from you, or one that has no special interest in you except that you render Him the service He requires of you. On the contrary, you must represent Him as visi-

bly present to you, as taking a kind and loving interest in all that concerns you, as true and faithful to His own solemn declaration: "As the Father hath loved Me, I also have loved you." You must make Him the center of your thoughts by a diligent study of His life, mysteries and teachings; of your affections by frequent acts of most fervent love; and of your actions by a faithful imitation of the example of a holy and virtuous life that He has given you. Reflect often on the plea for a return of love that He makes to you: "Abide in My love!", and resolve to surrender yourself unreservedly to Him, even as did His Apostles and first priests.

*Reading the Gospels.*

18. In striving to acquire a high degree of this personal love for Him, you will be greatly aided by the devout and meditative reading of the Gospels. Whenever you take up this sacred book and read any part of His instructions, imagine yourself among His Apostles who heard with their bodily ears these same instructions as they fell from His sacred lips. What impression, do you think, His teachings would have made upon your soul if you had been privileged actually to hear them as Peter and John and the rest of the Apostles heard them? Try to determine just what the final results of such a wonderful favor would have been in your case. You would have been one of those of whom our Lord said: "Blessed are the eyes that see the things that you see, and the ears that hear the things that you hear." But what would have been the net results of this special grace on your sanctification?

*Imaginary Results.*

19. No doubt you are convinced that His words would have worked wonders in your soul for the reason that it would simply have been impossible for you to resist the

71

power of His divine authority. You would surely have loved Him as did Peter and John and Martha and Mary! At His invitation to leave all things and follow Him, you would gladly have left home and parents and friends and the pleasant things of life, in order to attach yourself to Him and find your happiness in doing His bidding! Perhaps you have often wished you could have enjoyed this precious favor, and regretted that it is no longer granted to those who are preparing to become His priests and share the labors of His Apostles. You fancy that in a very short time you would be able to acquire a very high degree of holiness under the immediate direction of this heavenly Master of the spiritual life.

### A Mistaken Estimate.

20. But, strange as it may sound, you are likely to be mistaken. If His words and instructions as you meet them now day by day in the pages of the New Testament, in spiritual reading, in sermons and conferences, in the advice of your confessor or director, in the good example of your superiors and companions and of good lay people, do not produce any telling results in your spiritual life, you can safely conclude that they would not have produced any even if you had heard them directly fall from His sacred lips. More than this. Unbelievable though it may seem, it is nevertheless true that even His most astounding miracles would not have had the effect of making you abandon a life of tepidity and embrace one of wholehearted devotion to the perfect service of God.

### A Telling Example.

21. Do you doubt the truth of this statement? Here is the proof. Simply reflect on the sad career and death of Judas. He enjoyed the very same privileges and graces and favors that were granted to the eleven other Apostles. He had as true a vocation as they. Like them he had received

72

the power of working miracles, and very probably he actually made use of this power for the benefit of the afflicted. He listened to the same lessons of sanctity that the others listened to, and had always before him the most perfect Example of every Christian virtue. Yet see how, in spite of the fact that for no less than three years he was most intimately associated with the eternal Son of God made Man, his soul became gradually enslaved to sin and to Satan, and how his heart became so obdurate in wickedness that not even the most tender appeals of our Lord were able to bring about his repentance, conversion and salvation!

### "Neither will they believe."

22. We have it on the infallible authority of Christ Himself that nothing is to be hoped for in a man who is not influenced and converted by the word of God. When Dives in hell pleaded with Abraham that he send Lazarus to his five brothers to preach to them lest they be lost like himself, the answer given him was this: "They have Moses and the prophets; let them hear these and they will be saved." "No," counters the unhappy Dives, "this will not be sufficient; but if one were to rise from the dead and preach to them, they would be saved." And what is the answer? "If they will not hear Moses and the prophets, neither will they believe if one were to rise from the dead." Which proves clearly that not even miracles will be of avail with a man who refuses to turn the grace of God's own word to a good account.

### Spiritual Direction.

23. Let us now say a few things about spiritual direction. Since the path to holiness lies through the wilderness of one's evil inclinations, habits of past sins, spiritual blindness or defective vision due to such things as lack of clear knowledge of what is to be done, the deceptive

promptings of self-love, the natural dislike for the work
of overcoming difficulties, and especially the countless obstacles by which the enemy of salvation tries to block the
way, no seminarian can hope to make progress in holiness unless he has humility enough to submit himself to
the guidance of a counselor — a spiritual adviser or director — either in his confessor or some other priest. According to St. Bernard, he who would presume to undertake his own direction has a fool for a master and a fool
for a disciple. And a fool abounds in his own sense.

### "Go to Damascus!"

24. If then you would correspond perfectly with God's
designs for you and achieve success in the arduous work
of acquiring the sanctity demanded by your holy vocation,
you must have the humility to allow yourself to be guided
by a spiritual adviser. God has willed that souls should
largely be led to perfection through the aid of His repre-
sentatives. This truth is tellingly illustrated in the Acts
of the Apostles. St. Paul was converted by a miracle.
But he was not instructed about his mission in the same
way. When he asked: "Lord, what wilt Thou have me
to do?", he was told to go to Damascus and present himself to Ananias and receive from him the necessary in-
formation about his mission as an Apostle. Cornelius was
favored with the vision of an angel who told him that
he was to receive the gift of faith in answer to his prayers
and good works. But he was at the same time told to
send for St. Peter and be instructed by him in the truths
of salvation.

### A Dangerous Venture.

25. It happens sometimes that seminarians yield to the
temptation of being their own directors of conscience and
trying to steer their conduct by the smattering of moral

theology that they have picked out of their textbooks, or may have been taught by some of their companions who set themselves up as self-appointed guides of the souls of their fellow-students. Little do they suspect the grave risks they run by this dangerous practice. Self-love and self-interest will in every case dictate the decision, and in doing so will see to it that no violence is done to one's evil inclinations. Those who presume to be their own directors will be those who seek not the narrow and strait way "that leads to life," but rather the broad way "that leads to destruction"; for the real motive inspiring this self-direction is the desire to escape the painful process of self-denial and mortification that is essential for the acquisition of sacerdotal perfection.

*High and Low Ideals.*

26. It is a very deplorable fact that there are some seminarians who are guilty of the folly of self-direction, with the greatest harm to themselves and the souls to be entrusted to them later on. Instead of trying to *live up* to high ideals and serve God in the most perfect manner possible, they make use of the smattering of moral theology they possess to *live down* to the lowest level of morality short of mortal sin. They engage in the extremely hazardous experiment of deciding — in their own favor, of course — where lies the border-line between mortal and venial sin, and then acting on these decisions. This is every bit as dangerous as continually walking close to the edge of a deep precipice. No one can do so without sooner or later losing his balance or making a false step and falling into the abyss.

*Self-satisfied.*

27. Referring to one who does not take a serious view of his perfection, St. Augustine exclaims: "If thou sayest, It is enough thou hast perished." This has a closer prac-

75

tical bearing than may at first appear. For if one says, It is enough for me to keep out of mortal sin, this self-bestowed license to commit venial sin quickly demoralizes his reckoning about mortal sin. The priest or seminarian who steers his conduct by moral theology, which is so largely a manual of first aid to desperate sinners, will soon stumble on the brink of destruction. The one whose obligation to perfection is not only general, as is that of all Christians, but also special by reason of his state of life, as is that of the priest, and who instead of taking the maxims of the Gospel for his guide, prates about "common sense" as his standard, is marked for destruction.

### Interferences.

28. How much is one's progress in holiness hindered by persistence in some single unmortified practice, such as full indulgence of the appetite at meals (or between meals), waste of time and of mental force in newspaper and magazine reading, listening to the radio, or long talks with favorites? What effect has any *one* of these practices — for all of them taken together mean a hopeless spiritual malady — on such essential conditions as purity of intention, or love of prayer, or zeal for souls? According to spiritual writers, such unmortification, if habitual, or even if only of frequent occurrence, blocks advance all along the line and threatens retrogression. To serve God perfectly, one must practise vigilance with a particularity bordering on fanaticism.

### Rule of Generosity.

29. Hence you must by all means get away from the mistaken and fatal idea that all is well as long as you manage to keep out of mortal sin. Such a low ideal is unworthy any follower of Christ, let alone a seminarian, who is destined to be "another Christ." Nor will it do

to aim merely at avoiding the grosser venial sins. Your service of God must be a service of undivided love. Your conduct must therefore be regulated by the rule of *generosity*. This rule can be formulated thus: Resolutely avoid everything that you know to be displeasing to your divine Master, even though it may not be positively sinful; and generously do everything that you know to be pleasing to Him and that He desires you to do for Him.

## No Haggling with God.

30. If you follow this rule you will never haggle with Him as to what you are going to do for Him or give to Him. Your persevering aim from morning till night will be to do His will. You will not stand, as it were, with a balance in hand, trying to weigh continually what is commanded and what is forbidden under pain of sin, determined to avoid that, but equally determined to enjoy everything else that affords physical and sensual pleasure. If your love of Jesus Christ is what it should be, you will do much more than the commandments call for; you will make the precepts and maxims of the Gospel your rule of life. You must be able to say truthfully with Him: "I came not to do my own will, but the will of Him that sent me." Also recall these words: "If you keep My commandments you shall abide in My love; you are My friends if you do the things that I command you."

## Proportionate Holiness.

31. Whether you realize it or not, the fact remains that, having been called to the sacred priesthood, you are now placed under the strict obligation of sanctifying yourself to the very best of your ability. From the time you first became aware of the call to become one of God's chosen ministers it was your duty to strive earnestly and perseveringly after the holiness in keeping with the sublimity

of that office for which you are destined. But how have you responded to this duty in the past? Have you not perhaps reserved to yourself the right, so to speak, to lead a careless, easy-going and worldly life on the plea that the duty of striving after perfection is restricted to monks and nuns, and does not extend to those who are called to the diocesan priesthood? And what are you doing now in this matter?

*A Supposition.*

32. To dispel any wrong notions you may have on this head, and to convince you that you are under obligation to aim at the very highest degrees of holiness, we direct your attention to a very instructive passage in the *Following of Christ:* "If you had the purity of an angel and the sanctity of St. John the Baptist, you would not be worthy to handle this Sacrament." What food for reflection in this thought! Now it is plain that God does not expect you to possess a holiness as great as this on the day of your ordination, nor, for that matter, even on the day of your death. Supposing however that by a very special favor of God you did possess it, what a wonderful consolation it would be for you! So near to God and so pleasing in His sight! Surely God could then testify of you on the day of your ordination: "This is My beloved son in whom I am well pleased." But yet you would have to make this humble admission: "I am not worthy of so great a dignity."

*The State of Your Soul.*

33. A little self-examination is now in order. What is the actual state of your soul at this moment? Is it perhaps deeply scarred with the marks of past mortal sins? Have not your venial sins been as numerous as the sands on the seashore? Are you not ailing with the dangerous disease of tepidity? What use have you been making of

the many graces bestowed on you for the purpose of enabling you to fit yourself in every way, intellectually, morally, spiritually, for your exalted position? What are you doing to comply with the commandment of the love of God: "Thou shalt love the Lord thy God with thy whole heart and whole soul and whole mind and all thy strength"? And how are you observing the other equally important one: "Thou shalt love thy neighbor as thyself"; or better still: "This is My commandment, that you love one another as I have loved you"?

### The Possible Realized.

34. You cannot have the purity of an angel, nor the sanctity of St. John the Baptist, nor are you expected to have them. There is one thing, however, that strictly speaking, you could possess; and that is a degree of holiness perfectly commensurate with the many vocational graces that God has bestowed on you in view of your sacred calling. Thus it was possible for you to have preserved your baptismal innocence unstained and unspotted; to have avoided not only mortal sin, but also all deliberate venial sins; and in addition to this, to have practised in a heroic degree the various Christian virtues, such as humility, meekness, charity, self-denial, prayer, intimate union with God. It was possible for you to have employed all your graces to the best advantage and to have abused none of them. You *could* have done what, for example, we know a St. Aloysius did. And supposing you had done this, what a marvelous degree of holiness you would possess at this moment! And how more marvelous still would it be on the day of your ordination, if you persevered steadily in the path of virtue! Our Lord would then be able to testify that you were His beloved friend indeed, since you had acquired that degree of holiness which it was possible for you to attain with the graces granted to you for that purpose.

35. Remember that the striking feature about this supposition is that it represents what, strictly speaking, was possible for you to accomplish. Now contrast it with what is the actual state of your soul at this moment. Have you not every reason for the profoundest humility and the bitterest sorrow at the countless graces you have wasted and abused; the innumerable venial sins you have committed without the least hesitation; perhaps even very shameful mortal sins for which you have not tried to do adequate penance, having been satisfied with a confession that left much to be desired for thoroughness and the spirit of contrition? What has been your attitude toward the various amusements and pleasures that are so commonly an occasion of grievous sin to young people; and even apart from that, are inconsistent with the ideals that must inspire one destined to be a minister of Christ? Very likely honesty and humility compel you to strike your breast and confess: "Peccavi nimis cogitatione, verbo et opere" during all these years of preparation for what you know to be the sublimest dignity that can be conferred on the soul.

### More Joy in Heaven.

36. Surely the sight of so much sinfulness and of the neglect of self-sanctification should humble you to the very dust, and fill you with confusion and remorse. But at the same time you must not yield to discouragement. Your case is not hopeless, even though much sinfulness has marked your youthful life up to the present. The way to becoming a very holy and useful priest still lies open to you. Nay, if your repentance and conversion are very sincere and thorough; if you renounce sin completely and surrender yourself to God with your whole heart and soul; if you henceforth foster compunction and prac-

tise habitual penance for your sins; know that you will
be able to attain to a very high degree of holiness in a
very short space of time. You will be one of those whose
perfect conversion will give more joy to heaven than the
state of ninety-nine just who do not stand in need of
penance. And if your conversion is perfect, there is no
grace that God will deny you, and no favor that He will
refuse to grant to you. God's pardon of your sins is
absolute and final.

## Co-operation Essential.

37. But whatever may be the state of your soul — still
rejoicing in the grace of baptismal innocence, or recon-
ciled to God by wholehearted repentance — the fact that
you are called to be a priest implies that you are called
to be a holy priest. You are called to be as holy as it is
possible for you to become with the help of the graces
allotted to you. God does not impose an obligation on
you that is beyond your strength to fulfil. But He does
impose the obligation on you to do what lies in your
power. You must turn His graces to the best possible
account. This, as we insisted before, essentially requires
your faithful co-operation. The work that lies before you
is hard and exacting, no doubt about that; but it is not
impossible to one who is willing to work and determined to succeed. Set to work then with an earnest resolve to respond fully to God's loving intentions in your
behalf. Cultivate a burning desire to reach that particular
degree of holiness that He has appointed for you.

## Two Types of Priests.

38. There are two classes of men whom God is pleased
to select as His priests. The one class is typified by St.
John, the beloved Disciple, and the other by St. Peter,
the Penitent Apostle. St. John is the prototype of those
young men who have the happiness of entering the sacred

priesthood with their baptismal innocence unspotted and untarnished; while St. Peter is the model of those who had the misfortune of sinning grievously before their elevation to the sacerdotal dignity, but who, like him, have expiated their evil deeds by suitable works of penance. Both are called to an exalted degree of holiness. Both are destined to do much for the glory of God and the good of immortal souls.

### St. John the Innocent.

39. The former, like their model, St. John, are happy in the thought that by reason of their virginal purity they too are "disciples whom Jesus loves." The consciousness of this special love of their Master should be for them a powerful incentive to intense gratitude for the graces which alone enabled them during the dangerous years of youth to escape the ravages of sin, especially of lust. It should impel them to apply themselves incessantly to the work of sanctifying themselves daily more and more — "He that is holy, let him become holier still." It should inflame them with ardent zeal "to spend themselves and to be spent" in laboring for the promotion of their Divine Master's interests among the souls of men. A right understanding and just appreciation of the peculiar relation in which they stand to Him is enough to give them a foretaste of the surpassing happiness and bliss that awaits them when they shall be admitted into the unveiled vision of His glorified humanity in heaven.

### St. Peter the Repentant.

40. Those who have St. Peter as their model have no reason to be discouraged on account of their sinful past. They too can become, and are meant to become, very holy priests. In fact, their past sinfulness can become a wonderful help toward solid and heroic virtue. As God continually draws good out of evil, so can they do the same.

Cultivating an abiding sorrow for their sins and practising at all times the virtue of penance will accomplish this. St. Peter shows them the way. He profited much by his sin. It is certain that he loved His Divine Master much more ardently after his fall than he did before; and that the sorrowful remembrance of his sin made him far more zealous in his labors and far more willing to suffer for Christ than he would have been if he had not carried about with him that lifelong grief of heart over his triple sin. The abiding sorrow that he fostered the rest of his life imparted to his love a special quality that more than made up for his momentary lapse from grace. He now loved his Master more intensely and deeply, and rejoiced to suffer and lay down his life for Him. An encouraging example to a truly penitent priest or seminarian!

*Perfect Conversion.*

41. Hence an aspirant to the sacred priesthood who has had the misfortune to commit grievous sins in his youth has no reason whatever to feel discouraged, provided his conversion is genuine and perfect, and he practises the virtue of penance. (We except, of course, those who have been guilty of the sins that Canon Law declares to constitute an impediment to Sacred Orders.) But we repeat: the conversion must be a sincere one. This implies that he has not only confessed his sins with true penitence, but also that he has renounced them effectually, together with the voluntary proximate occasions thereof; and finally, that he is resolved to foster an abiding sorrow and practise lifelong penance for them. One who is truly penitent will never think that he has done enough penance and made adequate reparation. Hence he is not only willing, but even glad, to suffer for the cause of God, be it by sickness, poverty, failure, disappointment, humiliation, false accusation, persecution. He accepts these resignedly, and endures them in union with Christ's sufferings, both

83

for the purpose of atoning for his sins and of drawing down on his work the blessing of heaven. Moreover, he who keeps his offenses against God in constant remembrance and fosters compunction for them, will be faithful in all that relates to the duties of his office. He will be temperate, abstemious and unworldly; devoted to prayer and recollection and union with God; kind to his neighbor and forgiving to all who offend or injure him; fully convinced that what he suffers here by way of atonement is nothing compared with what he deserved to suffer hereafter. And so he is able to say truthfully with St. Peter: "Lord, Thou knowest all things; Thou knowest that I love Thee."

### *vercoming Obstacles.*

42. To sum up. Whether you are still in your baptismal innocence or have, like St. Peter, recovered the friendship of Christ by a perfect conversion, your present duty is to leave nothing undone to acquire the highest degree of holiness commensurate with the special graces that God offers you by reason of your vocation. Do not make the fatal mistake of underrating your obligation in this matter. Do not let the natural dislike that you feel for the hard work that lies before you prevail upon you to follow the line of least resistance. Do not allow the devil, the enemy of all that is holy, who is determined to ruin you at any cost, to persuade you that mere ordinary holiness is quite sufficient for you. And do not harbor the foolish thought that God is going to make an exception in your case, or is going to do some extraordinary or miraculous thing to rouse you to a realization of your obligation; or even that He is going to reward your negligence by bestowing on you the sanctity that He has decreed must be acquired by your own persevering efforts.

*Example of the Blessed Virgin Mary.*

43. Learn a very instructive lesson from the conduct of the Blessed Virgin Mary. She was destined for the sublimest dignity that could be conferred on any creature. But during the years of her infancy, childhood and youth she had not the slightest inkling of her vocation. She had not the faintest suspicion that she was chosen to be the Mother of God. Yet for all that, she was perfectly responsive to grace and faithful in preparing herself for her sublime dignity. Her co-operation with grace left nothing to be desired. All this was the result of her realization of what she owed to God merely because she was His creature. And so perfect was her preparation for her future dignity, of which she as yet had no knowledge, that she could not have made it more perfect even if she had been told about it in her childhood.

*A Contrast.*

44. What lesson are you to learn from this example? It is this: Mary knew nothing of her special vocation; yet from her earliest infancy she was perfectly faithful in her preparation for it. You have known for many years what designs God has for you. You are to share to a large extent the dignity of Mary. Yet what have you done, and what are you doing now, in the way of preparing yourself? Are you faithful to the graces given you? Are you striving to acquire freedom from sin? Are you drilling yourself in the virtues of your holy state? Are you cultivating recollection, union with God, the spirit of prayer? Are you "crucifying your flesh and its vices and lusts," and are you "crucified to the world, and is the world crucified to you" as the forceful language of St. Paul expresses the need of self-denial and mortification? If you had no foreknowledge of your vocation and its requirements, there might be some excuse for your remissness in striving

after the sanctification demanded of a future priest; but now that you know clearly what lies ahead, you have no justification if you neglect the work that God has given you to do.

### Love the Powerful Motive.

45. Taking now for granted that you fully realize that God has placed you under strict obligation to acquire a holiness suitable to your exalted vocation, you no doubt want to know how you must go about it in order to succeed in this responsible undertaking. The answer is not difficult. You must begin by cultivating a motive that will be both powerful and able to fill you with sustained enthusiasm. This is as necessary to you as the spring is to a watch, the roots to a tree. And this motive is nothing else than an *earnest and intense desire to become holy, springing from an ardent personal love of Jesus Christ.* These two must go together, though the former springs from the latter. If you foster a generous, whole-souled love for your Divine Saviour, you will also foster a strong desire to grow more and more pleasing to Him by holiness of life. The combination of these two will work wonders in your life and conduct. It will solve all your difficulties and problems. It will clear away all obstacles. It will make you shrink from doing the least thing which you know offends or displeases your Divine Friend; and it will make you courageous and even heroic in doing His will in all things, no matter how great a sacrifice this may demand of you. This personal love will make you dread the mere possibility of displeasing Him, hence make you determined to be always of one mind with Him. If you happen to commit a sin, you will at once hasten to ask His forgiveness and make atonement. If there is question of the propriety or impropriety of certain actions, as taking part in worldly amusements, you will decide by this rule: "A good seminarian will not do what his Master would

86

not do; and will not go where his Master would not go." In short, for one who fosters an ardent personal love of Jesus, all difficulties, trials and temptations are no hindrance, but rather so many additional helps, to great progress in the work of his sanctification.

*ormation of Character.*

46. Finally, there is the important work of *character-forming.* Unless you have formed a *character,* you will always be handicapped in your priestly life. You will be like the proverbial reed shaken with every wind. Now, a man of character is one whose life is dominated by *principles,* as distinguished from a life dominated by mere impulses from within and circumstances from without. Principles are conceptions deeply rooted in the mind, elevated into standards of judgment, taste, feeling and action, and consistently applied to life. And a collection of principles covering all departments of life constitutes an *ideal.* An ideal must be embodied in a set of definite principles dominating life; this will result in character. For a Christian, and much more for a seminarian, the model and ideal is Christ as manifested through His words and actions. This ideal has the advantage of appearing before him ready-made, in a concrete and living form, and is all the more calculated to influence him on that account. A seminarian, therefore, who has formed a character will know what he has to do and will do that faithfully, even in the face of difficulties — from a sense of duty, for the love of God and for his own sanctification. He will disregard the adverse opinions of men and not be swayed by human respect. He will resist the pressure of crowd-psychology; will never do any wrong or omit good to escape the censure of men; and never try to please men at the risk of offending God, to Whom he must one day render an account of his stewardship.

# BIBLIOGRAPHY

## PARTIAL LIST OF ASCETICAL BOOKS FOR SEMINARIANS AND PRIESTS

### 1. Spiritual Reading

| | |
|---|---|
| *The Eternal Priesthood* . . . . . | Cardinal Manning |
| *The Internal Mission of the Holy Ghost* . . . . . . . . . | "          " |
| *Sin and Its Consequences* . . . . | "          " |
| *The Love of Jesus to Penitents* . . | "          " |
| *Christ the Life of the Soul* . . . | Abbot Marmion |
| *Christ in His Mysteries* . . . . | "          " |
| *Union with God* . . . . . . | "          " |
| *St. Vincent de Paul, a Guide for Priests* . . . . . . . . | Leonard |
| *History of St. Vincent de Paul* . . | Bougard |
| *St. Vincent and Mental Prayer* . . | Leonard |
| *Dignity and Duties of the Priest* . . | St. Alphonsus |
| *Growth in Holiness* . . . . . | Faber |
| *Spiritual Conferences* . . . . | " |
| *At the Foot of the Cross* . . . . | " |
| *The Precious Blood* . . . . . | " |
| *The Ambassador of Christ* . . . . | Cardinal Gibbons |
| *The Young Priest* . . . . . . | Cardinal Vaughan |
| *The Minister of Christ* (two volumes) . | Bishop Vaughan |
| *Venial Sin* . . . . . . . . | "          " |
| *Thoughts for All Times* . . . . | "          " |

| | |
|---|---|
| *Priestly Virtue and Zeal* . . . . | Kirlin |
| *In the Likeness of Christ* . . . . | Leen |
| *Why the Cross?* . . . . . . . | " |
| *The Holy Ghost and His Work in Souls* . . . . . . . | " |
| *Progress through Mental Prayer* . . | " |
| *The True Vine and Its Branches* . . | " |
| *Introduction to a Devout Life* . . | St. Francis de Sales |
| *A Treatise on the Love of God* . . | " |
| *With Jesus to the Priesthood* . . . | Grimal |
| *At the Feet of the Divine Master* (four volumes) . . . . . . | Huonder |
| *The Priest's Way to God* . . . . | Plassmann |
| *The Curé of Ars* . . . . . . | Monnin |
| *The Priest of Today* . . . . . | O'Donnell |
| *Dominus Vobiscum* . . . . . . | Bishop Kelley |
| *Toward the Priesthood* . . . . . | Dubray |
| *The Priesthood* . . . . . . . | Bishop Stockums |
| *Considerations on the Priesthood* . . | Piot-Remler |
| *Practical Ascetics* . . . . . . | Smith |
| *The Art of Living with God* . . . | Bishop Busch |
| *Mary the Mother of Jesus* . . . | Willam |
| *The Holy Sacrifice of the Mass* . . | Cardinal Bona |
| *The Holy Sacrifice of the Mass* . . | Gihr |
| *An Epitome of the Priestly Life* . . | Arvisenet |
| *Practice of Christian Perfection,* by Alphonsus Rodriguez, translated by . . . . . . . . . | Rickaby |
| *Spirit of Faith* . . . . . . . | Bishop Hedley |
| *Lex Levitarum* . . . . . . . | " " |
| *Our Failings* . . . . . . . . | Von Oer |

The Holy Scriptures, especially the
New Testament, and the Sa-
piential Books of the Old Testament . . . . . . . . . .

The Following of Christ . . . . Kempis

## 2. Meditation

Meditations on Christian Dogma
(two volumes) . . . . . . Bellord

Meditations on the Life, Teaching
and Passion of Jesus Christ
(two volumes) . . . . . . Ilg

Meditations for Every Day in the
Year . . . . . . . . . Challoner

The Priest's Daily Manna . . . . Schmitt

Pusillum . . . . . . . . Fr. Athanasius

The Holy Eucharist in our Daily
Lives (Thirty-One Meditations) . . Cardinal Massimi

Meditations of St. Thomas Aquinas . McEniry

The Priest's Companion . . . . Marcetteau

## 3. Ascetical Theology

Theologia Spiritualis Ascetica et
Mystica . . . . . . . . . de Guibert

Introduction to the Study of Asceti-
cal and Mystical Theology . . . Goodier

Christian Perfection and Contemplation . . . . . . . . . . Garrigou-Lagrange

The Spiritual Life . . . . . . Tanquerey

Doctrine and Devotion . . . . . "

A Manual of Ascetic Theology . . Devine

90